A Pastoral Art

A Pastoral Art

Spiritual Guidance in the English Mystics

JULIA GATTA

Introduction by Kenneth Leech

Darton, Longman and Todd
London

First published in Great Britain in 1987 by
Darton, Longman and Todd Ltd
89 Lillie Road, London SW6 1UD

Originally published in 1986 as *Three Spiritual Directors* by
Cowley Publications
980 Memorial Drive
Cambridge, MA 02138, USA

ISBN 0 232 51740 1

British Library Cataloguing in Publication Data

Gatta, Julia
A pastoral art : spiritual guidance in
the English mystics.
1. Mysticism—England—History—
Middle Ages, 600–1500
I. Title
248.2′2′0942   BV5077.G7

ISBN 0–232–51740–1

Phototypeset by Input Typesetting Ltd, London SW19 8DR
Printed and bound in Great Britain by
Anchor Brendon Ltd, Tiptree, Essex

For
The Society of St John the Evangelist
Cambridge, Massachusetts

Contents

Abbreviations

Preface

The roots of this publication go back to the fall of 1978 when the Society of St John the Evangelist agreed to sponsor my fledgling ministry of spiritual direction. Under their guidance I began the long process of integrating my graduate study of the English mystics with the practice of contemporary direction. Because direction is an art, springing from the whole of oneself and taught above all by personal communication, I stand deeply indebted to the members of the society who have so shared themselves with me, and to the community as a whole, which has over the years welcomed me as a colleague, sister, and friend. For this reason I have dedicated the book to them.

Rowan Williams would probably be surprised to learn how much this study owes to his *The Wound of Knowledge*, which does not even discuss the English mystics. But more than any other work, his penetrating reading of ascetical writers has helped me grasp something of the divine paradox so vividly apprehended by Julian and the author of *The Cloud of Unknowing*.

At the heart of my work on the medieval mystics is the belief that they can continue to instruct us. This conviction is regularly confirmed for me at my parish, the Church of the Resurrection in Norwich, Connecticut, home of the recently established Order of Julian of Norwich. I am grateful to this community and to the guardian of the order,

Fr John-Julian Swanson OJN, for helping to recover the mystical tradition for the Church.

No one has shared in the labour of this book more than my husband, John. He has made his broad knowledge of the mystics and his considerable literary skill available to me at every stage of thinking and writing.

Introduction

'If then you are wise,' wrote St Bernard, 'you will show yourself rather as a reservoir than as a canal. A canal spreads abroad water as it receives it, but a reservoir waits until it is filled before overflowing, and thus without loss to itself communicates its superabundant water.'[1] It is the purpose of this book, I believe, to enable more of us to become reservoirs. For, as St Bernard goes on to remark, there are very many canals, and few reservoirs. There are many in today's Church who seem to do their theology as they go along, picking up scraps here and there, now and then, but who lack that rootedness in the 'great tradition' which is the necessary source for radical criticism and for the reawakening of the prophetic spirit. There is a desperate need for the recovery of spiritual depth, and this involves a reflective, though critical, encounter with the living past, with what Chesterton called the 'democracy of the dead'.

In recent years, in Britain and particularly in the United States, there has been a renewal of interest in the fourteenth century. Part of this renewal is certainly connected with the fact that the fourteenth century was, in so many ways, similar to our own day: plague, earthquake, popular risings, and resurgence of occult and pseudo-mystical groups, fears of the end of the world, and so on. In England the celebrations of the 600th anniversary of the Peasants' Revolt in 1981 coincided with the rebellions of urban black youth in Brixton and Liverpool. On 13 July 1981, Dr Allan Boesak, the South African leader, preached a sermon on the same spot, in Blackheath, South London, on which John Ball, the peasants' leader, had preached in 1381.

In the renewal of interest in the fourteenth century, the English mystics have been a focus of fascination, though also a cause of surprise. The paperback bookshops were taken aback in 1967 when, without warning, *The Cloud of Unknowing* suddenly became popular among the mystical wing of the hippy culture, people who had no interest in, or sympathy with, the institutional Church. When the 600th anniversary of Julian of Norwich's *Revelations* took place in 1973, Penguin Books had allowed their popular edition of Julian to go out of print!

Part of the fascination with the fourteenth-century mystics must be due to the fact that Western society has become a very unmystical and indeed unspiritual society. And this is not only true of society as a whole. The Church, deeply compromised and conformed within that society, shares and manifests its characteristic features. So we have a very activist, superficial and worldly Church, which has lost its roots in the historic tradition, or, where it claims to be 'traditional', has often mistaken tradition for conservatism and convention. Too often, 'traditional' Christians are found to be those who adhere to the conventions of an age just past.

It is in order to aid the renewal of a real encounter with the living tradition that Julia Gatta has written this study of the pastoral wisdom of three fourteenth-century mystical writers. In this important introduction to their work of spiritual direction, she has contributed to the present resurgence of interest in the classical tradition in pastoral care. Thomas Oden has written a good deal in recent years of the need for a pastoral theology which 'has turned again to the classical tradition for its bearings'.[2] It is this process which Mother Julia helps us to enter, a process which will help us to overcome that 'pervasive amnesia towards the classical Christian past'[3] which has been so harmful an influence in much twentieth-century pastoral strategy.

As a priest of the Anglican Church, Julia Gatta stands for a contemporary commitment to Christian discipleship which is rooted in the tradition of Catholic orthodoxy and the living spirituality of the mystics. She does not defend, or support, that nostalgia for an imaginary past which often passes for orthodoxy. Rather she points us to the need for a sense of solidarity with the past, with the spiritual guides of the past, as an essential element in our own journey, so different and yet so similar to theirs. In this book she has presented some valuable insights into the pastoral approach of three writers: Walter Hilton, Julian of Norwich, and the author of *The Cloud of Unknowing*. She brings out the importance of the affections (combined with a mistrust of excessive emotionalism) in Hilton, the earthy incarnational mysticism of Julian, the contemplative simplicity of *The Cloud*.

In reading this valuable book, I think we need to bear three things in mind. The first is the closeness of these writers of long ago to our own condition. It is very mistaken to assume that spiritual progress is chronological, and that, because of this, thinkers of an earlier age can be of no help to us. So much of the wisdom of the past speaks to our need. For example, a great deal of recent Western Christian theology since Paul Tillich has been concerned with the idea of God as the 'ground of our being'. It is vital that we recognize that this kind of thinking does not occur in a twentieth-century theological vacuum. The theme of God as 'depth' and 'ground' is a central one in many medieval writers, especially in those of the fourteenth century. For Julian, God is the ground, the substance, the very essence of nature, the true Father and Mother of natures. Our souls are 'deeply grounded in God' for God is 'the foundation in which our soul stands'. Again, there has been a good deal of attention in recent years, from Moltmann and others, to the theme of the 'crucified God' and the divine suffering. Here again Julian points to the centrality of the Passion in Christian mysticism. This is no 'flight of the alone to the alone', but a recognition of our essential unity with God in Christ, nourished and strengthened by the Incarnation and the Passion. For 'the most important point to apprehend in his Passion is . . . that he who suffered is God'. Again, in an age when there is, on the one hand, great doubt and bafflement about ultimate things, and, on the other, the frightening resurgence of new and crude fundamentalisms which leave no room for doubt and struggle, it is necessary to go back to that apophatic tradition represented by *The Cloud* within the West. *Agnosia*, unknowing, has a central place in Christian spirituality and ethics. Mother Julia will have done us a great service if she helps us to see the continuity and solidarity between these old Christian writers and our own continuing struggles.

A second truth which we need to remember is that any spiritual direction which claims the name Christian must look to and draw upon the rich tradition of spiritual writing and spiritual striving. One of the greatest errors of the present is to assume that any spirituality is better than none. But the spiritual world is not universally benign, and there are real dangers in exploring the spiritual realms, not least of mistaking the paranormal and the sensational for the spirit. The demand for spiritual direction, which has become something of an epidemic in parts of the United States, is an understandable reaction against consumerism. But it is all too easy to make 'spirituality' another commodity or product to be promoted within a social and political framework which is taken for granted. Private spiritualities, safe, unprophetic, wholly inward, are very popular, and shady charlatans have surfaced who are only too eager to offer 'spiritual direction' – in exchange, of course, for the appropriate fee. The demand for direction within the Churches has come at a time when perhaps they were least equipped to provide it. A Church which has ceased to pray, ceased to challenge the principalities and powers, and become concerned more with the provision of comfort than with transformation, is in a weak position to guide. So I hope that Julia Gatta's book will push seekers after God back to explore the Christian spiritual tradition which belongs to them.

The tradition is important, however, because it is a 'living tradition': it is not a fossilized tradition, which we simply repeat and reproduce. So, thirdly, there needs to be a critical, prayerful, contemporary encounter and dialogue with the past which can enable us to move towards the Christian future with hope and a sense of progress. We can only do this if we are a future-oriented people, a people on the move, a pilgrim community. But a pilgrim people is aware of where it comes from, and it is this sense of rooted-ness in past vision and past encounters which makes the journey into the living darkness possible. Julia Gatta has uncovered some of the riches and insights of the mystics of the fourteenth-century Church at a time when the Church is at its least mystical. But the recovery of an authentic Christian mysticism is one of the greatest needs of our day. In Karl Rahner's words, 'the Christian of the future will be a mystic, or he or she will not exist at all'.[4] My hope is that this important book will help towards the recovery of the mystical life within the twentieth-century Church.

KENNETH LEECH

1   St Bernard, *Sermons on the Song of Songs*, 18:2.

2   Thomas C. Oden, *Care of Souls in the Classic Tradition* (Philadelphia: Westminster Press, 1984), p. 37.

3   Ibid., p. 11.

4   Karl Rahner, *The Practice of Faith: A Handbook of Contemporary Spirituality* (London: SCM Press, 1985), p. 22.

1

A Way into God

Therefore every scribe who has been trained for the kingdom of heaven is like a householder who brings out of his treasure what is new and what is old. (Matt. 13:52)

It falls to each generation of Christians to dispense the treasure of the gospel. Again and again the Church re-presents the faith from her ancient treasury, enriched always by new gifts in every age. The effective dispersal of this immeasurable wealth depends, in part, upon 'training for the kingdom of heaven' and, presumably, knowledge of what is stored up in the treasury. Moreover, the able householder needs to have developed some way of ascertaining which of his master's treasures are needful, and when.

Over the centuries the Church has fulfilled an aspect of this vocation through the practice of spiritual direction. It is a demanding ministry. Like the scribe commended in the gospel, directors must undergo spiritual training, possess a wide knowledge of their religious heritage, and be endowed with the gift of discernment. A branch of *pastoralia*, spiritual direction embraces those charisms described in the New Testament as prophecy, discernment of spirits, and teaching. While all these gifts are present in the Church for a variety of purposes, their use in spiritual direction is rather specific: to help individuals recognize God's particular ways with them. In this process, the old gifts of

7

the treasury – the apostolic and universal faith – are brought to bear on a unique life. Then, too, the Spirit's new gifts are discerned and named and so appropriated. In the complex dynamic of spiritual direction – the interplay between old and new, universal and particular, God and the soul – directors stand in the middle. They are called to be faithful both to the one whose stewards they know themselves to be, and to the members of the household of faith committed to their charge.

Given the rigours of this ministry, it is not surprising that modern spiritual directors find themselves daunted at times by the task set before them. Indeed, because this work so obviously depends upon God, they are all but driven to frequent and earnest prayer. Yet even more than prayer is required. Those who undertake the direction of others must themselves be under direction, usually for some years. For this ministry is an art transmitted from one person to another. They will also need to study to know the treasure itself: the powerful but elusive Word of God found in Scripture, tradition, and the human heart.

Fortunately, we possess some record of those who have struggled before us to know God and to lead others to him. The writings of holy men and women, the spiritual directors of ages past, have themselves become part of the store of wealth we can draw upon to relieve our spiritual impoverishment. In these works we can discover a large fund of wisdom born of vivid encounter with God, deep self-knowledge, and years spent in the cure of souls. This is particularly true of the writers who form the basis of this book: Walter Hilton, Julian of Norwich, and the anonymous author of *The Cloud of Unknowing*.

The contribution of each of these three to Western mysticism is today generally recognized, but why study them together? True, they all lived in England at roughly the same time in the late fourteenth century, but there is no proof that they either knew one another personally or were acquainted with the others' works. The concerns which immediately prompted their writings are clearly dissimilar. Hence, they cannot be said to constitute a 'school' of spirituality in any formal sense.

Yet among these three diverse personalities, there exists a common spiritual temper. Their writings are broadly learned, but not pedantic; impassioned, but not over-wrought. Each employs homely metaphors and colourful turns of phrase to convey challenging theological ideas. They eschew everything fussy, eccentric, or histrionic. They do not burden themselves or others with an excess of rules. All their own searching, all their pastoral advice, moves toward a single goal: union with God.

These, then, are pastors who are first mystics – men and women whose guidance of others is centred upon God. This is the overriding passion of their own lives and they assume its presence in their readers. They remind us that what prompts spiritual direction must be the desire for God. Direction cannot be a forum for personal culture, whether in medieval or modern guise – programmes for the cultivation of either virtuous living or self-fulfilment.

These mystics have tried to transmit something of their experience of living on close terms with God in the form of ordered spiritual counsel. While all their writings, especially Julian's, contain elements of personal history, they are primarily works of spiritual direction rather than mystical autobiography. At the distance of six centuries, it is sometimes hard to know precisely what audience each had in mind. Hilton and the *Cloud*-author address several of their works to unnamed individuals, but recognize that they will be read by others, too. Julian states simply that God communicated with her through visions for the sake of her fellow Christians. Yet in her own time the *Revelations* does not seem to have been widely circulated. In view of

9

the small number of manuscripts surviving from the Middle Ages, and the growing readership for the *Revelations* today, it would seem that Julian's book was destined more for the twentieth century than for the fourteenth.

When I call these writings works of spiritual guidance, I am not of course suggesting that we have at our disposal anything like transcripts of actual conversations. The literary genres employed by the mystics are in fact quite complex; and for that reason, all the more interesting and rewarding to read. Their pastoral art is woven into a rich textual fabric that includes strands of theological exposition, keen psychological description, actual and imaginary dialogue, and expert handling of such devices of literary artistry as allegory, parable, and metaphor. All this is held together by their delightfully concrete Middle English prose, whose pungency survives even translation.

The immediate aim of their efforts is educational. Hilton's *Scale of Perfection* has been dubbed a 'summa' of the interior life. Julian considers her revelations a 'blessed teaching' to be passed on to others. *The Cloud of Unknowing* presents a method of dark contemplation and expounds its underlying theology. Each writer labours to broaden our theological horizons. In this regard they do not really contradict contemporary trends in spiritual direction that emphasize religious experience, rather than ideas, as the proper focus of spiritual direction.[1] For the English mystics would agree that the ultimate purpose of direction is engagement with God. Their writings, however, remind us of the necessarily corporate setting in which this encounter takes place. A slow and painstaking process, growth in the spirit depends in part upon our gradual appropriation of our common religious heritage. Knowledge of the theological tradition of the Church, and the practice of her spiritual disciplines, are not addenda to our relationship with God. They open the door more widely to the Spirit and help us interpret God's movements as they occur. Given the limited time and specific focus of spiritual guidance, contemporary directors often cannot furnish directly the theological and ascetical education their clients require. Still, the example of the English mystics would suggest that at least some provision be made for this kind of formation.

The mystics' attention to the theological dimensions of direction are also related to their exercise of discernment. At various points in their writing, each is concerned with interpreting certain affective states. Hilton examines emotion under many aspects: religious fervour and dryness, sweetness and remorse, our feelings of love, joy, anger, and dread. Julian probes the problem of spiritual despondency. The *Cloud*-author delves into the psychic pain encountered in negative prayer. In handling any particular emotion, they first describe the sensations it provokes with astute psychological insight. But experience, no matter how accurately delineated, can never furnish its own interpretation. For this, they draw upon the wide tradition of the Church. Only when our experiences are situated within their larger theological context can we begin to grasp their spiritual import and ultimate meaning. By communicating something of their theological vision, the mystics assist our discernment of these same feelings in ourselves.

The English mystics are somewhat at variance with modern sensibilities in the degree of their attention to the problem of sin. It may be that, on the whole, our medieval forebears look too readily for a moral answer to life's evils, and we for a therapeutic one. But in the case of these writers, simplistic solutions of either sort are rejected. They perceive the psychology of sin with penetrating shrewdness; but they appreciate, too, the extent of our helplessness before it. They are utterly free of moralism: the deadening reduction of the spiritual life to ethical probity.

If sin is so complex and intractable, why then do they

11

bother about it? Sin demands attention to spiritual guidance because, as core resistance to God, it inevitably impedes union with him. As the *Cloud*-author puts it, 'If you had God then you would be without sin, and if you were without sin then you could have God'. The persistence of sin therefore defeats the mystics' deepest longing, and is an occasion of frustration and sadness.

Hence these and other mystical writers explore the way of 'purgation': the process by which God gradually purifies and frees us. At every stage it involves some degree of human cooperation. All our mystics assume their readers follow the traditional course of ascetical discipline: regular prayer, reflection upon one's state of conscience, and sacramental confession as needed. Their audience would be composed of those already trying to shape their lives on the pattern of Christ. The Middle Ages produced many popular handbooks designed to help such people understand and recognize sin. These works explained the seven deadly sins and their contrasting virtues; they offered advice on resisting the former and cultivating the latter. To some extent, Book One of Hilton's *Scale* belongs to this genre.

For the most part, however, our mystics press the next step: what to do when human striving has reached its furthest limit, but still falls short of the goal. Julian struggles with the depression that sets in at this point, and is eventually brought to see how even sin is 'necessary' to the completion of God's plan for us. Hilton traces our purification through its several phases, from the early stages of deliberate effort through the radical purgation whereby God liberates us at a depth beneath consciousness. The *Cloud*-author insists we relinquish ourselves to this passive purification through the strenuous exercise of negative prayer.

What we can do, then, when our own efforts fail is

entrust ourselves to God, and learn to recognize the signs of his activity within us. Undergirding the mystics' treatment of purgation is neither a Pelagian confidence in human self-perfection nor a Calvinist pessimism about human depravity. The mystics approach purgation with a strong faith in God's power – and intention – to restore human nature to its original goodness. In fact, they believe still more. Sin actually contributes to God's ultimate purpose: a perfecting of creation that incorporates tragedy, evil, and pain. The purgation of which the mystics speak is not, then, an attempt to recover primeval innocence, but a way of letting God establish the 'new creation'. Theirs is a spirituality of transformation.

Through their pastoral art – and, by extension, their literary art – the mystics seek to impart some sense of this ongoing transformation. Every aspect of their counsel, for instance, is informed by a theological anthropology: the conviction that human nature mirrors God's own. The biblical conception of our creation in the image of God, together with St Augustine's psychological interpretation of this *imago Dei*, define for them the essence of what is 'natural'. Sin is a hard fact of existence, but it is contrary to human nature because it distorts this divine character. The mystics draw us into a universe in which not sin but only God is our final horizon.

Just as the mystics' visionary perspective unfolds the hidden glory of human nature, so it expands our apprehension of God. For Julian and the *Cloud*-author, the experience of Christ crucified reveals God's self-emptying nature, his connection to creation through affliction. In Julian's visions of the Passion, and in the painful exercise of dark contemplation recommended in *The Cloud*, the startling truth of divine love is made manifest. Each of the three mystics approaches this mystery in a distinctive way. But in the end, all their ways converge upon Christ, whose humanity is itself the way into God.

1   William A. Barry and William J. Connolly, *The Practice of Spiritual Direction* (New York: Seabury Press, 1982), p. 8.

2

Walter Hilton
and the Religious Meaning of Emotion

In the late fourteenth and fifteenth centuries, there was in England no more highly esteemed devotional writer than Walter Hilton, author of the massive *Scale of Perfection*. The appeal of this masterwork over the centuries owes much to the exceptional breadth of Hilton's teaching. So wide and capacious is the *Scale* that almost any reader can find a place in it: Hilton teaches the rudiments of prayer as well as the highest reaches of contemplation, the initial steps of conversion as well as the final degrees of purgation.

Between these poles the author charts an interior course that consists not so much of a rigid step-by-step formula for spiritual ascent as a broad, yet detailed, description of our entire movement towards God. He delineates what is for him the crucial process of 'reformation in faith and feeling' with enough psychological precision to be helpful, yet without overwhelming the reader with minute, idiosyncratic diagnoses.

That Hilton's guidance *is* useful may be deduced both from the popularity he enjoyed in his own day, as indicated by the numerous extant manuscripts of the *Scale*, and from his continuing reputation in later generations. His esteem was only enhanced by the invention of printing. For when Wynken de Worde produced an edition of the *Scale* in 1494, Hilton became the first English mystical writer ever to appear in print. Though the *Scale* continued to be republished as late as the nineteenth century, it was Evelyn

Underhill's 1923 semi-critical edition that established Hilton as a master of the mystical way.

Yet we know very little about Hilton's life. His North Midlands dialect has prompted scholars to suppose he was born somewhere in Yorkshire. After ordination to the priesthood, he studied for a mastership in canon law at Cambridge. He may have practised his profession for a time in the diocese of Lincoln. Inspired perhaps by the example of William Flete, the English disciple of St Catherine of Siena, Hilton eventually abandoned his ecclesiastical career and instead became a hermit. His earliest treatises date from the period of solitude. But for some reason, whether of physical constitution or of spiritual temper, Hilton found himself unsuited to the eremetical life. He subsequently entered the Augustinian Priory of St Peter, Thurgarton, Nottinghamshire, where he remained until his death in 1396.[1]

Hilton was a highly prolific writer. Besides the *Scale*, he wrote several letters and short treatises in both English and Latin, and made perhaps as many as three translations of devotional writings.[2] Many of these works, and certainly his letters, seem to have been produced in response to specific requests for spiritual guidance. Such evidence shows Hilton to have been an experienced spiritual director, whose personal counsel was evidently much in demand.

What we can know of Hilton's pastoral art has to be deduced from these writings, and especially from *The Scale of Perfection*. Though the textual history of the *Scale* is somewhat obscure, it is evidently comprised of two books written at different times and for slightly different purposes. Book One is addressed to a female recluse, though Hilton no doubt composed it, like Book Two, with a larger audience in mind: the devout middle and upper class laity and the numerous members of religious orders who sought experiential union with God. The first book is primarily an ascetical work, centred on moral preparation for contemplative prayer. Book Two, considered a work of Hilton's maturity, deals at greater length with contemplation itself and presupposes a more theologically sophisticated audience.[3]

Throughout the entire range of the *Scale* the author presents himself, above all, as a teacher. And like all good teachers, Hilton wants his pupils to grow towards greater independence from him. To foster theological maturity, he lays deep theoretical foundations in his direction. Again and again he sets forth the reasons underlying his specific advice. He expects his readers to internalize those spiritual principles that will help them interpret their varying situations for themselves. He prompts us to consider how our own experiences and aspirations fit within the tradition he presents.

THE AMBIGUITY OF EMOTION

The most characteristic function of spiritual direction is what has been called the 'discernment of spirits': the interpretation of the diverse religious impulses to which human beings are subject. The kinds of spirits that may influence us are traditionally categorized as three: the Holy Spirit, the demonic spirits, and one's own spirit. It is a sensible schematization. Our everyday experience tells us that we are moved by good and evil forces, and by some that are morally neutral, which arise from our own psyches. Yet at times it may be difficult, especially for the person undergoing them, to distinguish these spirits from one another.

The discernment of spirits has occupied the Church since her earliest days. For St Paul, the 'ability to distinguish between spirits' is a particular charism given by God to certain individuals for the common good (1 Cor. 12:10). 'Do not believe every spirit,' writes the author of 1 John, 'but test the spirits to see whether they are of God.' The criteria for such testing is, first of all, consonance with the faith of the Church. John goes on to explain how his readers can begin the process of discernment: 'By this you know the Spirit of God: every spirit which confesses that Jesus Christ has come in the flesh is of God, and every spirit which does not confess Jesus is not of God' (1 Jn 4:2). Writing to Christians under pressure from gnostic groups, the author presents belief in the incarnation of Christ as the criterion by which they can distinguish true from false prophecy. Discernment, then, has a necessarily theological foundation.

It also has an emotional basis. The fruits of the Spirit that Paul enumerates – love, joy, peace, patience, and so forth – are fundamentally affective states. One of the ways we can determine whether an impulse or action is of God is by examining its emotional effect on us. In his classic 'Rules for the Discernment of Spirits', for example, St Ignatius Loyola makes particular states of emotion – desolation and consolation – the starting point for discernment. Such an emphasis on affectivity as an essential ingredient of human personality is, of course, remarkably harmonious with major trends in modern psychology.

Throughout his writings, Hilton plays out the several senses of affectivity at each stage of the spiritual life. 'What is a man but his thoughts and his loves?' he asks, echoing Augustine (I, 88).[4] The whole self is engaged in the process of union with God. Both our minds and our feelings have to undergo conversion, progressive purification, and finally transformation. But intellectual renewal, if not easy, is at least a relatively straightforward matter compared with the redemption of affectivity. For emotion, especially religious emotion, is a complex phenomenon. The fruits of the Spirit

18

cannot be equated simply with 'feeling good'. There is a false feeling of consolation that can lull us into complacency and inertia. Likewise, we can undergo spells of desolation that coexist with a sense of peace deeper than surface emotion. By themselves, our emotions remain an unreliable index of our state of soul before God, but at the same time they cannot be ignored.

Because of the centrality of affection in Hilton's scheme of interior progress, one can elucidate the whole of his thought by attending to what he means by 'affectivity' and seeing how he guides his readers through its complexities. Then, too, his handling of the problem of affectivity has value, as Hilton himself would want to say about all good theological thinking, that is practical as well as theoretical. Popular movements of religious enthusiasm, whether the 'free spirits' of the Middle Ages or the charismatics of our own, are apt to measure spiritual authenticity on the thermometer of feverish zeal. Even those acquainted with ascetical principles are prone to judge their love for God and neighbour by its emotional fluctuations. Every spiritual director knows how easily the spiritual life is confused with states of emotion, and yet how crucial for spiritual and psychological development are both emotional discipline and healthy emotional expression.

In every age, affectivity poses a dilemma: how can we pursue prayer that is emotionally engaged without becoming dependent upon particular affective states? How do we gain a measure of freedom from our vacillating feelings without cutting them off from the process of redemption? How are our affections sanctified, and how do we manage them in the meantime? Hilton's response to the ambiguity of human emotion is as many-faceted as the problem. His treatment entails neither an uncritical endorsement of states of emotion, whether religiously inspired or not, nor an equally simplistic rejection of all intense feeling. Like every other aspect of human nature, affectivity needs to be interpreted, disciplined, and ultimately redeemed.

It is worth pausing here to note that for his anthropology Hilton, like our other English mystics, drew on the Augustinian 'faculty psychology' that was commonly held in the Middle Ages. According to Augustine, the image of God impressed on human nature manifests itself as a 'created trinity' composed of three psychological functions: mind, reason, and will. Each of these terms, for Augustine and subsequent tradition, implied a richer scope of activity than they ordinarily do in modern usage. 'Reason', for example, means more than the ability to think logically. It embraces all intellectual endeavours, including reflection, meditation, and intuition. 'Will' is the power by which we make choices and implement our desires; but here again the concept is wider than its modern analogue. To medieval thinkers, 'will' enables us to orient our lives existentially, and, above all, to love. 'Mind' is the most elusive and comprehensive term of all. It incorporates the psychological components of reason and will, yet contains even more: the mysterious, uncharted depths of human psyche. Finally, medieval psychology maintained that these 'higher' faculties of mind, reason, and will were inextricably linked with the 'lower' faculties of sensation and imagination, which depended directly on the body for their operations. As our capacity to love and to feel, affection in its various phases depends upon will and sensation.

Thus when Hilton speaks of the process of sanctification as a transformation of these faculties – including affection – he is not suggesting that we relate to God solely through conscious thoughts, decisions, or feelings. On the contrary, because these capacities are situated in the 'soul', they include what we would today call the unconscious as well as the conscious dimensions of the human person. While

Hilton and his contemporaries did not of course delineate the unconscious with the terminology or precision of post-Freudian psychology, they recognized the existence of powerful, inexplicable, and irrational forces, of which we are often unaware and which impinge upon thought, feeling, and behaviour.

Since the days of the desert hermits, Christian ascetical teaching has stressed the critical importance of self-knowledge for spiritual growth. Hilton draws upon this tradition when he recommends exercises in introspection. By this means one deliberately probes not only obvious manifestations of virtue and vice, but also, and even more significantly, one's hidden, underlying motives. In a way not wholly dissimilar from the techniques of modern psychoanalysis, material is thereby raised from the unconscious to the conscious mind, to be recognized and acted upon. When in his treatment of affectivity Hilton insists that we define ourselves in terms other than our feelings, it is not because he underestimates their significance. It is rather that he sees there is more to human nature than what we feel or consciously know about ourselves. Faith maintains the existence of a transcendent self, made in the image of God, beyond immediate sensation or apprehension. Hilton's resolution of the dilemma posed by our emotions consists in showing how our felt experience – so often at odds with this deepest identity of ours – can be brought into harmony with it. Such is the formidable and delicate task he undertakes in his direction.

INTERPRETING EMOTION

The redemption of emotion begins, paradoxically enough, by denying its religious ultimacy. Hilton often deprecates feeling as a reliable gauge of spiritual progress. Holiness is not guaranteed by fervour any more than inner stagnation

21

is necessarily evidenced by dryness. If there is any moral dimension to emotion, it consists in the response we make to it; and the response Hilton regularly recommends is a form of detachment. Unless we somehow distance ourselves from our feelings, they tend to assume a false and destructive absoluteness.

The emotional detachment Hilton advises is neither psychological suppression nor Stoic apathy. His ideal is not indifference, but a sense of perspective. Rather than have us anaesthetize our feelings, Hilton asks only that we see them for what they are: ever shifting materials for discernment. In themselves, they bear little religious import, for God judges not our feelings but our intentions. In every case, it is the response that we make to our emotional situation that matters, and that reveals our fundamental orientation for or against God.

If holding such an ideal of emotional asceticism causes Hilton occasionally to dampen the enthusiasm of the zealous, more typically it allows him to comfort those suffering from emotional or mental afflictions. Addressing the problem of persistent distraction in prayer, for example, Hilton gently advises, 'Abide grace, suffer easily, and break not thyself too much' (II, 24). Detachment in this case means accepting, provisionally at least, what we cannot change about ourselves. To assume responsibility for involuntary thoughts and emotions provokes a false sense of guilt and needless anxiety which, in the end, only distracts us from the real opportunities of grace around us.

Minimizing the significance of fervour in prayer is of course comforting to those undergoing dryness and distraction. To those naturally disposed to ardent and gratifying prayer, Hilton will apply the same principles but to a different end. In their case, he will show how genuine love for God implies obligations that may end up restraining their devotion. For instance, he cautions against artificially

22

prolonging consolations or insights that arise during meditation. They shall 'turn to pain and to bitterness' if we hold them too tightly, refusing to let them pass away as gracefully as they came. Hilton also places crucial external restrictions on the exercise of devotion. He reminds us that Christian prayer takes place in a communal context of social responsibility. When meditations become so absorbing that they impede manifest duties towards others, they have to be forcibly broken off. In the same way, we must curtail devotions that regularly disrupt sleep or eating, threaten our physical well-being, or pass beyond a 'reasonable time' (ML, 30–31).[5] Desire for God is lived out within a mesh of external obligations which define our relationship to him more accurately than powerful, though isolated, subjective experiences.

By demythologizing religious affection, Hilton tried to modify the excesses practised by followers of Richard Rolle, the celebrated hermit of Hampole. A vividly poetic and mystical soul, Rolle claimed to have experienced *calor, dulcor, canor* – 'warmth, sweetness, and melody' – in time of prayer. His disciples, however, interpreted his metaphors literally, and then strained to produce these same psychosomatic effects in themselves. Like the *Cloud*-author, who exposes these would-be mystics to merciless satire, Hilton rationalizes Rolle's metaphors without attacking the saintly hermit by name. Hilton explains that when physical sensations happen to accompany prayer, whether 'in sounding of ear, or savouring in the mouth, or smelling at the nose, or else any sensible heat as it were fire glowing and warming the breast', they are not to be counted as 'very contemplation' but merely the side-effects of it (I, 10). Such sensations are at best only the natural accompaniments of prayer, and at worst a diabolical temptation: for the devil can simulate these same impressions for his own malevolent purposes. Hilton therefore cautions against ever seeking physical sensations for their own sake or as a proof of the authenticity of our prayer.

The issue of possible psychosomatic disturbances in prayer occupies a short treatise of Hilton's called *Of Angels Song*.[6] This work is addressed to someone who, apparently aware of Rolle's claim to have heard angelic song, asked for some criteria by which true spiritual sensations might be distinguished from false. In his response, Hilton implies that the whole matter of emotional and physical phenomena has been greatly overrated. Perfection consists not in special religious feeling, but in the 'union of God with man's soul through perfect charity' (AS, 15). True, the restoration of human nature in Christ embraces body and soul, including emotion and sensation. Someone far advanced in grace might indeed be able to enjoy communion not only with God, but with angels and other spiritual beings in the communion of saints. Still, warns Hilton, this is a rare occurrence.

More common are cases of self-induced visions and voices. If not checked, these delusions cause great harm and can even end in madness. They are apt to occur when someone becomes ambitious for spiritual adventure and, leaving behind the ordinary path of prayer, Scripture reading, meditation on Christ, and self-reflection, 'violently gathers his wits together to seek out and gaze upon heavenly things. . . . He overstrains his wits with imagination, and with immoderate effort turns the brains in his head. . . . Like man in a frenzy, it seems to him that he hears and sees what nobody else does, but it is all just an idle fantasy' (AS, 18). So it is both more prudent and more humble simply to remove oneself from reliance upon fervent emotions and extraordinary sensations. For himself, Hilton declares, 'It is enough for me to live principally in faith, and not in feeling' (AS, 20).

When extraordinary phenomena do accompany prayer,

however, how can we determine whether they arise from
benevolent or sinister influences? Hilton offers the
traditional answer: by their moral consequences. We
cannot judge the quality of our prayer simply by assessing
the feelings it produces in us, in isolation from changes in
our behaviour or relationships. If powerful sensations are
sent by God, they will be confirmed in the course of time
by the fruits of the Spirit they unfailingly produce (I, 11;
LH, 235).[7] In any case, it is better not to depend too much
on the strength of our own religious experiences, but to
trust instead in 'the merits of Christ in the faith of the
Church' (LH, 235). The way out of the confusion caused
by vehement religious emotions is simply to refuse to rely
on them, one way or another.

When Hilton dramatizes the uncertainty of subjective
impulses on the one hand, he usually points out the
reliability of certain objective criteria on the other. The
discernment of spirits requires finding some dependable
points of reference outside oneself by which the spirits can
be judged. For the author of 1 John, the requisite theological foundation for discernment was the confession of
Christ's coming in the flesh. Hilton's understanding of faith
naturally reflects the greater elaboration of doctrine that
had taken place in the Church by the fourteenth century.
To distinguish the spirits from one another, and to prevent
unguided enthusiasm from degenerating into delusion or
heresy, Hilton insists that we constantly refer our spiritual
impressions back to their corporate foundation in the
Church. By bringing our ideas and feelings against some
external standard – namely, their congruence with Christian belief – we can test their authenticity: 'In the work of
the spirit your heart travels a true circle when it both
begins from and returns to the faith of the Church' (LH,
234).

Hilton's precautions are not groundless. Perhaps the

greatest danger to mysticism comes from within, in its own proclivity towards individualism and eccentricity. At its best, Christian spirituality stresses the necessarily communal dimension of personal holiness in a life marked by agreement in faith, corporate liturgical prayer, and mutual service. Even those called to physical solitude, such as hermits or recluses, experience their essential solidarity with other Christians through participation in the liturgy and intercessory prayer. The literature of the desert fathers and mothers of the third and fourth centuries, who were the classical solitaries of monastic history, extols social virtues – fraternal charity and mutual forbearance – as telling signs of holiness.

In the fourteenth century religious individualism took a wide variety of forms, but the heretical Free Spirits and Lollards perhaps represent its most troubling manifestations. Their appeal to earnest Christians, as Hilton seems to recognize, lay precisely in their claim to a spirituality superior to anything possible in the visible Church. The Free Spirit movement had originated on the continent during the previous century. Based in pantheistic mysticism, it advocated an absolute perfectionism that allowed its practitioners to abandon all their obligations and the common Christian fellowship of liturgy and sacraments. It also advocated quietism, the cessation of all human effort in the spiritual life, as well as anti-nomianism, the transcendence of moral, ecclesiastical, and civil law by 'the perfect'. Behind its facade of mystical rhetoric, one was apt to find the ugly realities of pathological vice.[8]

More common in England during this period were the disturbances set in motion by the Oxford professor John Wycliffe. An extreme philosophical idealist, Wycliffe denied the authority of the institutional Church and the validity of her sacraments. In many respects he revived the ancient Donatist heresy by asserting that sinful ministers endered the sacraments null and forfeited their own authority. His subtle arguments about the nature of Christ's presence in the Eucharist seem to have been interpreted by his supporters and enemies alike as tantamount to a denial of that presence. His followers, called Lollards, promulgated a popular form of his ideas that was often enough merely a vehicle for anti-sacramentalism and anti-clericalism. To counter the bogus mysticism of the Free Spirits and others like them, and to offset the Lollards' dismissal of the visible Church, Hilton stresses the need for adherence to the articles of the Creed, the sacraments of the Church, and the teaching of the early fathers (I, 21; LH, 234).

Yet there is another, more immediately pastoral motive behind Hilton's stress on doctrinal assent: namely, the firm ground of comfort and encouragement found in the very content of Christian faith. In both his *Letter to a Hermit* and the *Scale* Hilton is sensitive to the misgivings about salvation that can arise when people begin to perceive their frailties. After leading a correspondent through a strenuous exercise in self-examination, Hilton's first care is to address any temptation to despair that might come about through a heightened sense of personal sin. The devil, cautions Hilton, likes to play upon our anxieties about our state of soul, causing needless fears about salvation. Hilton therefore urges 'faith in the articles of the creed, and especially this one – the remission of sins' to counter his attacks. Here the Creed acts as an exterior source of assurance to stabilize the anguished perception of personal sin and to offer an objective reason to hope for salvation (LH, 233).

The ascetical importance of faith as intellectual assent also appears in Hilton's conception of 'reformation in faith'. In Book Two of the *Scale* Hilton divides the process of spiritual renewal into two phases, which he calls 'reformation in faith' and 'reformation in faith and feeling'. The first is accomplished relatively easily and quickly, since it consists simply in the sacramental restoration of our likeness to God through baptism or penance. But the full course of renewal, as we shall see, involves a profound liberation of the personality, affecting even our involuntary 'feelings'. Those who have undergone only the first phase and are still labouring to be 'reformed in feeling', will continue to experience the painful inner struggle dramatized by St Paul in Romans 7 (II, 11). The first reformation simply cannot penetrate the depths of the emotive self even though one 'may well feel sorrow for his sin, and a turning of his will from sin to cleanness of living'. For a new convert, all the old instincts remain intact, including darker, subliminal passions: 'For he is as he was unto his feeling, and he feels the same stirrings of sin and the same corruption of his flesh in his passions and worldly desires rising in his heart, as he did before' (II, 8). If we listened only to the testimony furnished by our feelings, we would have to conclude that nothing significant occurs in baptism or sacramental confession.

It is precisely because at this stage we usually cannot perceive grace within ourselves that faith here plays a critical role. Citing Romans 5:1 ('We are justified by faith') and other Pauline texts, Hilton argues that it is 'by faith' that we know ourselves to be saved when our interior dispositions do not yet testify to the change wrought by sacramental restoration: 'The righteous man lives in faith. That is, he that is made rightful by baptism or by penance he lives in faith' (II, 9). In so far as the distinction Hilton draws between the 'reformation in faith' and the 'reformation in faith and feeling' corresponds roughly to the theological difference between justification and sanctification, Hilton may be said to advocate a species of 'justification by faith'. But unlike classical Protestant formulators, Hilton sees faith in God issuing immediately in faith in the sacraments. He argues not against a false justification by works, but against a false justification by feeling. Salvation does not depend on a particular set of conversion experiences, but 'on faith'.

But if faith sometimes requires us to believe in our salvation despite the pull of contrary feelings, there are other times when our emotions contribute to our spiritual encouragement by indicating the movement of grace within us. Hilton, in fact, never denies the force and internal veracity of feelings as they are palpably experienced. But he does insist that emotion be viewed theologically, since raw experience is never self-explanatory. Just how skilfully Hilton weaves together compassionate acceptance of a client's own testimony about his condition with an objective sacramental and moral theology can be seen in one of his letters of direction, the so-called *Epistle to a Christian Friend Newly Turned to Our Lord Jesu*.[9]

The problem Hilton is tackling here is this: a friend fears that his sins remain unforgiven despite his recourse to the sacrament of penance. He does not entertain any scepticism about the effectiveness of confession as a sacrament; what he doubts is his own ability to make proper use of it. He complains that he cannot make his confessions specific enough: some sins, such as pride, are so pervasive that he can confess them only generally; others were committed so long ago that he can no longer recall their circumstances. But what gives all these anxieties terrifying force is his experience of continuing remorse. Because his sorrow for sin is as great after confession as before, he feels compelled to the alarming conclusion that he has not been absolved after all, despite his good intentions and best efforts.

Hilton's friend has advanced a 'theological' argument based on emotion: he is not absolved because he continues to feel remorse. Hilton counters this depressing line of thought with a theological argument which, while not centred on emotion, none the less takes emotional experience into account, and offers an alternative explanation for his friend's feelings. He begins with some useful theological distinctions. Conversion, or turning to God in contrition and love, he explains, does not spring from natural human volition but from 'grace alone'. Since one of the unmistakable signs of this grace is compunction of heart – 'the which tokens if thou hast them thou feelest them, so that they may not be hid from thee' – his friend has reason to take comfort. His deep remorse, far from indicating a lack of grace, is in fact the result of grace bestowed. He would not feel the contrition he does if God had not already touched him: 'By these tokens thou shalt trow steadfastly that grace is infused into thee, and by virtue thereof steadfastly trow that all thy sins are forgiven thee by grace' (CF, 453).

What about the sorrow that persists even after absolution? Hilton interprets this in terms of what medieval scholasticism called the 'effects of sin'. He explains that even after we have confessed our sins and been forgiven, there remain in us certain inevitable after-effects. Absolution cannot undo our sinful habits, which have perhaps developed over an entire lifetime. Nor can it free us entirely from conscience pain – the stinging remembrance of our wrongdoing. Yet these long-term consequences of sin can, in a sense, cancel each other out, because enduring the aching memory of past sins can be purifying. If his friend will patiently undergo the smarting of his newly sensitized conscience, the appeal sin once held for him will eventually diminish. Little by little his inclinations and habits will tend away from sin and towards God. And so, as moral purification deepens, he will discover a fresh sense of inner freedom. Still, Hilton does not minimize the psychological pain involved in this process: it is a trial passing 'many other sensible pains in this life'. Yet precisely because it is a 'shadow or likeness of purgatory', it presents an opporunity for spiritual cleansing (CF, 506). Hilton shows how he condition that had cast his friend into confused dejection opens an avenue to further growth. What looked at irst like a spiritual dead end turns out to be the very path o God.

A brief work written for someone facing a particular piritual crisis, the *Epistle to a Christian Friend* epitomizes Hilton's pastoral method at its best. Undergirding his pecific advice lie principles of spiritual direction that are till valid and helpful. Hilton begins the process of discernment by attending carefully to his correspondent's own estimony about his inner state. In this letter Hilton accepts ully his friend's account of his sorrowful feelings. Sensations such as these form the substance of what is to be discerned, and all real discerning has to start with ust such an empirical basis. If clients cannot furnish this necessary but often inarticulated evidence by themselves, lirectors need to help draw it out.

Direction, however, aims for more than the verbalization of religious experience. What is presented as a personal event still requires interpretation. This is where theological liscernment comes into play. In his *Epistle to a Christian Friend* Hilton, while regarding his friend's self-description as an accurate reflection of his feelings, none the less lisagrees with his explanation of them. His correspondent supposes that his sense of remorse indicates divine lispleasure: Hilton thinks just the opposite. To convince him that there is another way of interpreting the 'data' of his protracted contrition, Hilton brings theology to bear on his case.

Once discernment has uncovered the stirrings of grace at work in his friend, Hilton turns to exhortation. Theological liagnosis is not an end in itself, but helps us perceive how we can respond more fully to God. Instead of regretting and resisting the sorrow for sin that he feels, his friend could allow himself to undergo it – now with confidence that God can use it for his good. The general goal of direction – deeper union with God in the varied circumstances of life – is thus made possible in the particular case. A way is cleared for Hilton's friend to cooperate with divine grace.

As a paradigm of spiritual direction, the *Epistle to a Christian Friend* presents a threefold process. The first step involves accepting and eliciting religiously significant experience. Once this experiential content is established, a theological interpretation can be attempted, based on the director's familiarity with ascetical theology. Unlike the first stage, this aspect of direction is decidedly 'judgemental'. While experiences have to be regarded as irreducible facts of personal history, their meaning is open to interpretation. This is the specific task of discernment. Raw feelings are never self-explanatory. Turned in upon themselves they bring on presumption or, as in the case of Hilton's friend, despair. By mediating something of the Church's theological tradition, directors widen their clients' religious horizons while providing the interpretative principles necessary for discernment. This, in turn, allows a freer response to the grace that is now perceived and named.[10]

THE TRANSFORMATION OF EMOTION

In spiritual direction affectivity is sifted and discerned. If we are honest with ourselves and our directors, we begin to see how often our emotions are at odds with our moral and religious aspirations. 'Many a man,' writes Hilton, 'has virtues . . . only in his reason and in his will, without any spiritual delight in them or love for them.' We may know what is right and be disposed to do it, but none the less experience 'grouchiness, depression, and bitterness' as

32

we go about it (I, 14).[11] In Hilton's terminology we are reformed in 'faith' but not yet in 'feeling'. Do we have any reason to hope that our feelings might actually change over the course of time?

In *The Scale of Perfection* Hilton describes ways by which affectivity is gradually integrated with our fundamental orientation towards God. This 'reformation in faith and feeling' is a work of grace: humans can at most cooperate with God in it. Sometimes our participation will be active; at other times, a mere passive 'letting be'. The kind of response we can make to grace will therefore vary according to circumstances. But whether Hilton counsels expressing our emotions or reining them in, he sees the ultimate recovery of affectivity as an aspect of our redemption. It is part of the human wholeness we are destined to enjoy in Christ.

The process of transformation begins with conversion. As Hilton charts the typical course of the interior life, our emotions are first purified by using them in passionate affective prayer. Even at this early stage, we enjoy some foretaste of integrated prayer as emotion and will, though not yet intellect, unite in a concerted outpouring of affection towards God. The usual object of our impassioned love is, appropriately enough, the figure of Christ. Imaginative meditations on the life or passion of Jesus – or still other reflections on the attributes and acts of God – can provoke the whole gamut of religious emotion: love, joy, dread, reverence, contrition, and so forth. Though frequently exhausting, affective prayer is none the less cathartic and, in its own way, gratifying (I, 5; 30).

According to Hilton grace, not just human emotionality, fuels affective prayer. One called to it is strongly, though inexplicably, drawn to the 'savour, delight, and comfort, that he findeth therein' (I, 5). When we are still heavily dependent upon emotion, affective prayer brings God close to our experience. But its greatest value, as Hilton sees it, is purgative. The first of affectivity 'burneth and wasteth all fleshly loves and likings in a man's soul' (I, 31). Sin is cut off 'with the blissful sword of love' (I, 30). Holy passions cleanse unholy ones.

Affective prayer gives scope to emotion by channelling it towards God. Initially, it instils the desire for God through passionate love. In time, however, this desire presses deeper, past surface emotionality, to take hold of the will. Hilton regards the development of a stronger, more serious, but less emotionally charged 'desire for Jesus' as a mark of spiritual progress. It also signals the commencement of a long process of purgation, one that will cleanse more effectively than even the fires of affective prayer.

Before we can recover our emotions, they have to pass through an experience which Hilton describes under the metaphor of 'night'. As we shall see, this 'night of the soul' is not identical with the intellectual darkness urged by the *Cloud*-author, though it shares some of the same purifying effects. For Hilton, the night spans the whole interior life from our first determined efforts at contemplation until our attainment of it. It characterizes, in one phase or another, the interior state of most Christians who have given themselves to the pursuit of contemplative prayer. Like our earlier engagement with affective prayer, entrance into the night springs from 'great desire and yearning for to love and see and feel Jhesu' – only now we are unable to make contact, or so it seems, with the object of our desire. Instead, we find ourselves pulled away from God emotionally and intellectually by other things: anything, in fact, that has the capacity to preoccupy us can constitute an obstacle to God.

Hilton's advice on distractions in prayer fits naturally into his counsel regarding the night. Those whose thoughts wander afield during prayer, he assures us, should not suppose their devotions are thereby rendered worthless. What counts in prayer is neither fervent emotion nor even focused attention, but the will to pray. Hilton suggests that we begin praying with our desires integrated – 'make thine intent and thy will in the beginning as whole and as clean to God as thou mayest' – and then let come what may (I, 33). If we are overwhelmed with distractions, it is pointless to be angry with ourselves or impatient with God. The constitutional weakness we experience when reduced to such straits is an occasion for humility – a matter of more consequence for spiritual growth than ease in devotion. Anticipating John Chapman's famous dictum, 'Pray as you can, don't pray as you can't', Hilton exposes the futility of trying to force prayer. A steady turning towards God is what really matters, not immediate facility in prayer and meditation.

Hilton's 'night of the soul' describes the spiritual no man's land occupied by those who have withdrawn from the 'false light' of deliberate sin, but who cannot yet enter the 'true light' of contemplative vision. But the spiritual night, like its natural counterpart, admits of distinct phases. According to Hilton, entry into the darkness is the most painful stage of all, because there we are least familiar with the night. As we move deeper into it – and thus further from the 'false light' – the pull of former attachments gradually loosens. When moral struggle begins to subside, energies are freed to concentrate upon God: 'When thy soul through grace is made so free and so mighty and so gathered into itself . . . that it may without hindrance of any bodily thing think of right nought: then it is in a good darkness' (II, 24). While the *Cloud*-author might consider meditation on 'right nought' an apt exercise in dark contemplation, Hilton regards it as only a preparation for contemplative prayer. In this hour of the night we are consumed with the singleminded desire for God, yet without possessing him.

The spiritual night purifies emotion by denying it gratification. Hilton insists that we relinquish every attempt to satisfy our diminished affections and instead cling to God solely in the strength of our wills. Yet his emphasis upon will at this juncture is not an invitation to assert our egos. On the contrary, the crucial activity taking place in the night is effected by God rather than the self: 'Jesus Who is both love and light is in this darkness. . . . He is in the soul as its labouring for light in desire and longing, but He is not yet in it as its resting in love' (II, 24).[12] We cooperate with this divine action simply by holding ourselves available to it. Hilton thus recognizes that there is more to us than what feeling – or the absence of feeling – happens to call to our attention. Our emotional state alone cannot define us. For the sake of our whole human nature, we have to act upon our intrinsic identity as creatures made in the image of God, even when this runs counter to our felt sense of ourselves. By exercising our wills in surrender, we allow God to transform us in the subliminal depths beyond the reaches of consciousness.

The advent of contemplation comes by degrees. Exploiting an ample range of images traditionally applied to the mystical life, Hilton portrays it as a 'light darkness', 'rich nought', 'waking sleep of the spouse', 'burning in love', 'opening of the ghostly eyes', and 'reforming in feeling' (II, 40). Some of these metaphors underscore the paradoxes of contemplative experience: that one feels simultaneously humbled, yet wonderfully fulfilled; ignorant, yet possessed of an inexplicable wisdom. Other images suggest the maturing of earlier approaches to God through knowledge and love. Because the mind as well as the affections have been purged by the interval of spiritual darkness, both faculties have been rendered more capable of enjoying God. Intellectually, contemplation affords an intuitive knowledge of God through vision. It is not that we can ever see 'what God is' in this life; but contemplation allows us to perceive 'that he is'. Nor is this a coldly cerebral insight, for the contemplative is 'comforted and enlightened by the gift of the Holy Spirit with a wonderful reverence and a secret burning love, with spiritual savour and a heavenly delight' (II, 32).[13] Such a conjunction of contemplative wisdom with contemplative love marks not only a ripening of knowledge and affection, but also a full integration of one's human personality.

Critics have rightly pointed out that the 'reformation in faith and feeling' principally affects what Hilton, along with medieval philosophy generally, called the *ratio superior*, the 'over part of reason' – that is, mind, reason, and will.[14] The 'lower' faculties of sensation and imagination, through which emotion operates, are not involved in the act of contemplation and therefore remain relatively untouched by it. Yet the reformation in faith and feeling does bear upon emotion, as its very name suggests. In the spiritual night affectivity gains a quiet intensity. No longer is affection liable to revert to religious 'enthusiasm', nor to expressing itself in the ardent sentiments of its earlier passion. Once love has 'boiled out' the impurities of the soul through fervour, it 'clears, settles, and is still' (II, 29).[15] Because love is deeper it is less conspicuous.

The gift of love is the consummate gift of contemplation. Hilton explains that the power by which we now adhere to God is not our own natural affection, but 'Love unformed' – the Holy Spirit. In contemplation, God is 'both the giver and the gift'. As this love gradually takes hold of us, the virtues follow in course, without strain or effort on our part: 'For the soul does not strive as much to obtain these virtues as it did previously. Instead, it obtains them easily and experiences them peacefully' (II, 36).[16] The Holy Spirit thus refashions us from within.

Hilton is able to account for so radical a change in psychologically convincing terms. In his analysis of the process of sanctification he shows how the truth of God's goodness and love – a truth now apprehended with unprecedented clarity – floods the field of consciousness and measures all things in relation to God. Humility, for example, arises spontaneously when one sees 'how Jhesu is all and that He doeth all'. A fundamental shift in identity occurs when one perceives God as the centre of the universe and of oneself. The superficial ego of ordinary consciousness gives way at last to an apprehension of self that recognizes God as one's deepest and truest identity. Those grasped by this vision instinctively lose self-regard and the tendency to compare themselves with others, so absorbed are they in thinking about God (II, 37).

The love of God engendered by contemplation uproots sin in much the same way. As we are progressively released from the constraints of disordered feeling, we come to an inner peace so profound that it spills over in psychosomatic effects, creating a sense of physical repose along with inward stillness and contentment (II, 29: 40). All these fruits of contemplation – physical, moral, intellectual, and emotional – witness to an abundance of grace that restores the image of God and brings to perfection all aspects of our human nature.

Near the conclusion of the *Scale*, Hilton allows himself to be asked whether, in his endorsement of the 'new gracious feelings' that arise from contemplation, he has not retracted his earlier advice that we practise indifference towards religious emotion since 'the just man lives by faith'. He replies that while we ought never to seek 'bodily feelings', it is proper to desire the renewed dispositions that constitute reformation in feeling. Unlike the tangible sweetness and physical ardour of the neophyte, the recovered affectivity of the contemplative springs from a unified moral sensibility inspired, in turn, by the vision of God. Anyone who has had such an impression of God, declares Hilton, cannot help desiring it always (II, 41).

In his handling of the problem of emotion, then, Hilton's pastoral strategy is two-pronged. In the first place, he wants us to see that our spiritual state is not simply identical with our emotional state. Feelings, whether of fervour or of desolation, cannot tell us who we are before God. To uncover the meaning of particular affections we first have to subject them to theological discernment, usually with an experienced spiritual guide. Only then can we begin to see what response to our feelings God might be asking from us. For we are not just hapless victims of our emotions, but responsible participants in the work of divine grace. Discernment issues in an enlarged sense of personal freedom, which allows us to collaborate with those impulses that come from God and resist others that draw us away from him. If we cannot change our feelings, we can at least determine our attitude towards them.

Yet it is precisely such a change in our feelings that we most desire. Just as Julian is impatient for her own sanctification, so Hilton realizes that holiness must be the final term of grace. Salvation has to affect the whole personality. God's forgiveness eventually releases us at the profound levels of affectivity where sin has its source – in our spontaneous impulses of anger, envy, pride, and so forth. So while Hilton insists that God does not condemn us for whatever unmanageable feelings we now experience, we can none the less look forward to having 'virtues in affection' at the end of our course 'when, by the grace of Jesus and spiritual and physical exercise, reason is turned into light and will into love' (I, 14).[17] This transformation is what Hilton understands by the reformation in faith and feeling.

Hilton's balanced approach to affectivity neither ignores nor exaggerates its importance. Unlike our post-romantic culture, Hilton maintains that we are more than the sum of our feelings. When our emotions fall out of harmony with our deepest convictions and aspirations, Hilton consoles us with the reminder that our human nature is created in God's image – whether we happen to experience this at the moment or not. Our moral and religious posture is determined not by what we feel, but by what we desire and do. Although distancing ourselves from an 'affective identity' in this way may seem unnatural at first, in the end it preserves human freedom. Our emotions in fact present us with choices: not whether to have them – because that is outside our control – but whether to identify with them, harness them, or resist them.

Hilton's treatment of human emotion is a form of gospel, and for that reason can still be appropriated by spiritual directors. It is strangely liberating to grasp the relativity of emotion in a culture such as ours, which is so oriented towards personal experience. It is even more liberating to be presented with the prospect of emotive transformation, and in his pastoral art Hilton shows how affectivity itself moves towards redemption. His hopeful expectation of spiritual progress for those who cooperate with divine grace is characteristic of the catholic tradition of spirituality. Even our most distressing feelings, such as those Hilton analysed in the *Epistle to a Christian Friend*, or the desolate absence of feeling that marks the spiritual night, can be turned to our ultimate profit. Nothing need be lost, and in the end affectivity is purified and renewed as an integral part of our human nature.

For the sake of our intrinsic conformity to God's image, Hilton sometimes requires us to separate ourselves from our feelings. This ascetical advice is eminently practical, but Hilton does not delve into its theological foundation. He knows that it works, but does not explore why. For Julian of Norwich the 'why' will be crucial when she takes up a specific affective problem – that of spiritual despondency. Her meditations on the pain and glory of Christ will begin to answer that question.

1   Joy Russell-Smith, 'Walter Hilton and a Tract in Defence of the Veneration of Images', *Dominican Studies*, 7 (1954), 184–7. Helen Gardner, 'Walter Hilton and the Mystical Tradition in England', *Essays and Studies*, 22 (1937), 113. Phyllis Hodgson, *Three Fourteenth-Century English Mystics* (rev. edn London: Longmans, 1967), p. 32. J. P. H. Clark, 'Walter Hilton in Defence of the Religious Life and the Veneration of Images', *Downside Review*, 103 (January 1985), 1–2.

2   For a survey of the writings attributed to Hilton, see Alfred C. Hughes, *Walter Hilton's Direction to Contemplatives* (Rome: Pontifical Gregorian University, 1962), pp. 10–17. Clark, above, has recently shed more light on Hilton's canon and career with his study of some of the unpublished Latin treatises.

3   Even though Books One and Two of the *Scale* do not always appear together in manuscripts, it is evident from his introductory remarks to Book Two that Hilton intended it to be a continuation of Book One, despite the lapse of time in between. It may be that a later editor first brought the two together under their present and in some ways inappropriate title, for Hilton employs ladder imagery only once to describe the gradual, cumulative nature of spiritual growth (II, 17).

4   *The Scale of Perfection*, ed. Evelyn Underhill (London: John Watkins, 1923). Unless otherwise noted, book and chapter citations from the *Scale* are taken from this edition. In a few cases I have replaced Middle English words with their modern equivalents.

5   Chapter citations are from the *Mixed Life* in the *Minor Works*

of Walter Hilton, ed. Dorothy Jones (New York: Benziger Bros., 1929), pp. 3–77.

6   Page citations are from *Angels' Song* in *Eight Chapters on Perfection and Angels' Song*, trans. Rosemary Dorward (Fairacres, Oxford: SLG Press, 1983), pp. 15–20.

7   Page citations are from a *A Letter to a Hermit: Epistola ad Solitarium*, trans. Joy Russell-Smith, *The Way* (July 1966), 230–41.

8   Gordon Leff, 'The Heresy of the Free Spirit', *Heresy in the Later Middle Ages, I* (Manchester: University Press, 1967; New York: Barnes and Noble, 1967), pp. 308–407. J. P. H. Clark, 'Walter Hilton and "Liberty of Spirit" ', *Downside Review*, 96 (1978), 61–78.

9   Page citations are from the *Epistle to a Christian Friend Newly Turned to our Lord Jesu*, ed. Clare Kirchberger under the title 'Scruples at Confession', *Life of the Spirit*, 10 (1956), 451–6, 504–10.

10   For a developed modern treatment of the process by which we arrive at discerning knowledge see Bernard Lonergan, *Insight: A Study of Human Understanding* (London: Longmans, 1957; Darton, Longman and Todd, 1983; New York: Harper and Row, 1957).

11   *The Stairway of Perfection*, trans. M. L. del Mastro (Garden City: Doubleday, 1979).

12   Del Mastro trans.

13   Del Mastro trans.

14   Conrad Pepler, *The English Religious Heritage* (St Louis: Herder, 1958), p. 416. Gerard Sitwell, 'Walter Hilton', *English Spiritual Writers*, ed. Charles Davis (Tunbridge Wells, Kent: Burns and Oates, 1961; New York: Sheed and Ward, 1961), p. 32.

15   Del Mastro trans.

16   Del Mastro trans.

17   Del Mastro trans.

3

Passion and Compassion
in Julian of Norwich

As a young woman, Julian of Norwich prayed for a deeper sense of Christ's Passion. By apprehending the crucifixion physically, through a vision presented to her senses, she hoped to participate in Christ's suffering through compassion. Her prayer was answered when, at the age of thirty, she underwent sixteen visions or 'showings'. As she lay stricken with a near fatal illness, a crucifix set at the foot of her bed seemed to come alive. Over the course of the next day and a half, Julian engaged in remarkable verbal exchanges with Christ while a series of arresting images were presented for her meditation.

Little is known of Julian apart from the book she wrote to preserve this experience, *The Revelations of Divine Love*. We do not even know her true name, for 'Julian' is almost certainly a religious name, taken from the church of St Julian and St Edward in Norwich where she eventually became an enclosed anchoress. Julian dates the revelations herself – 13 May 1373 – but the circumstances of her life at this time are obscure. Whether she was then, or ever, a nun remains a mystery. For while the church of St Julian and St Edward belonged in the fourteenth century to a Benedictine priory at nearby Carrow, there is no definitive evidence to show that Julian was herself a Benedictine. Some details supplied by the *Revelations*, such as the presence of her mother and her parish priest at what was thought to be her deathbed, would tend to suggest her engagement in secular life at the time of her visions. From the slender evidence supplied by references to her in contemporary wills, however, we can determine that she was established as an anchoress by 1394 at the latest, and was still living in 1416.[1]

The anchoritic life which Julian embraced differed from the solitude of hermits. While a hermit might roam from place to place, an anchoress was geographically restricted – bound, in fact, to remain within a single dwelling. Anchorholds varied in size from a single cell, often attached to a church, to a suite of rooms with an enclosed garden. Julian, like hundreds of other anchorites in medieval England, would have spent most of her day alone, engaged in prayer and quiet forms of handwork. But one window of her anchorhold would have faced the outside world; through it she was available to her 'even cristen', as she called them, for spiritual guidance.

According to her contemporary, Margery Kempe, Julian enjoyed a reputation as an astute spiritual director.[2] Those who sought counsel at her cell window, as Margery did, found her expert in matters of discernment. In *The Revelations of Divine Love*, it is evident that the same pastoral wisdom for which Julian was renowned in fourteenth-century Norwich is available to us in the document she left to succeeding generations.

JULIAN'S SENSE OF AUDIENCE

The Revelations of Divine Love has survived in two forms, both written by Julian. She probably composed the briefer version not long after the visions themselves.[3] This version represents a fairly straightforward account of the showings, a skeletal rendition of the events of 13 May: what she saw and what was said. The later version, with which this chapter is concerned, is about three times longer than the

44

earlier one. Besides offering a narrative of her visionary experience, this account renders the fruit of Julian's twenty years' reflection upon the meaning of the showings.

Because it describes an intense religious experience, the *Revelations* could be classified as a species of mystical auto-biography. But Julian clearly wrote for others, not for self-expression. The sixteen visions that form the theological foundation and narrative framework of the *Revelations* were not, according to her, either a special spiritual privilege nor a divine ratification of her personal sanctity, but a 'blessed teaching' (73).[4] Early in the *Revelations* she protests that the visions were granted only so all might be stirred to greater love of God: 'Everything I say about me I mean to apply to all my fellow Christians, for I am taught that this is what our Lord intends in this spiritual revelation' (8). Julian thus serves in the *Revelations* as a representative type, a spiritual everyman.

And yet, it is not quite everyone whom Julian represents. There is a limit placed on her representative function for, as she repeatedly asserts, the revelations pertain only to those 'who will be saved'. But are there any who will not be saved, any for whom the *Revelations* is not intended? We cannot know – at least not from Julian's book. Although Julian is plainly troubled by the prospect of damnation for anyone, and wonders how eternal separation from God could ever be reconciled with God's promise that 'all shall be well', the problem of damnation is left an open question by the revelations. They do not contradict the traditional teaching of the medieval Church; they simply do not address the question. Julian declares that the visions pertained only to those who would be saved: 'God showed me no one else' (9).

But even if the revelations are only for the elect, Julian's implied audience is still somewhat narrower in scope than all those destined for eternal joy. Towards the end of the

Revelations, in Chapter 73, she tells us whom she is addressing, and why. Her book is for 'such men and women as for the love of God hate sin and dispose themselves to do God's will'. Her intended audience, then, consists of those traditionally called 'proficients' in the Christian life: not those on the brink of conversion, nor at the beginning of a dedicated Christian life, but those who have earnestly lived the faith for a number of years. Such persons yearn to make spiritual progress: to be free of sin and attraction to evil, and to experience union with God to the furthest degree possible in this life, through contemplative prayer. Such a person we may assume Julian was, as were many who sought her counsel at her anchorhold window.

What is the particular need of this group? Certainly not an exhortation to make an initial commitment in faith, because for these people such a dedication is already part of their personal history. No, what proficients typically need are grounds for continued perseverance in hope. Impatience, discouragement, and despair are the noonday demons most apt to tempt those somewhere between conversion and consummation.

According to Julian, these souls suffer from two kinds of sin or sickness. The first is impatience or sloth, the classical capital sin of *accidie*. Sloth refers not so much to physical idleness (though it may come to this) as to a spiritual malaise, expressing itself emotionally as despondency, listlessness, and loss of heart. Those attacked by it no longer find any point to disciplined effort, since the results of such effort are practically indiscernible. And they may be stirred to angry impatience with themselves or with God for this unpromising state of affairs.

The other failing to which 'God's lovers' are most liable is what Julian calls 'despair or doubtful fear'. This second sin would be an outgrowth of the first, for despair is the terminal point of accidie. Here we would have embraced the anxious pessimism raised by our initial misgivings. In the end, despair or doubtful fear undermines faith: faith in God's love, God's fidelity, and his intention to bring us to sanctification and glory.

These are the only particular sins mentioned in the course of the *Revelations:* 'He showed sin generally', writes Julian, 'but he showed no sins in particular but these two . . . which most belabour and assail us' (73). It is worth noting, moreover, that neither of these sins springs from anything imaginary, delusional, or necessarily neurotic. They are, in clinical terminology, 'reality-based'. Temptations to accidie and despair are occasioned by nothing other than our true perception of our moral and spiritual failures. The spiritually ambitious who observe their lack of progress inevitably feel discouraged: 'Sin is the sharpest scourge with which any chosen soul can be struck', observes Julian (39). And she notes that the seeds of our discontent are sown in the very process of conversion:

> When we begin to hate sin and to amend ourselves according to the laws of Holy Church, there still persists a fear which hinders us, by looking at ourselves and at our sins committed in the past, and some of us because of our everyday sins, because we do not keep our promise or keep the purity which God has established us in, but often fall into so much wretchedness that it is shameful to say it. And the perception of this makes us so woebegone and so depressed that we can scarcely see any consolation (73).

But how can we maintain hope in the face of the overwhelming evidence to the contrary: the magnitude of evil in the world and the stubborn persistence of sin in ourselves?

For Julian, it is 'ignorance of love' that keeps us in despair. The visions God granted her, the teachings she passes on, are concerned with countering this ignorance with revelations 'of divine love'. In her final chapter, Julian declares simply, 'Love was our Lord's meaning'.

Yet Julian does not categorically pronounce the *fact* of God's love as a proposition to be believed. Instead, she gives full play to doubt and difficulty before situating painful experience in its largest theological context. She avoids premature closure on problems by first dealing with the intellectual and affective obstacles her readers were likely to face. Julian thus moulds theodicy – the attempt to understand how divine goodness and justice can be squared with the existence of evil – in an emphatically pastoral design. She makes its abstract, speculative character concrete by involving herself existentially in those vexing problems of sin and providence that she knew lay beneath temptations to spiritual depression. By exposing her struggle with Christ over the problem of sin, Julian acts as a theologian of fierce intellectual honesty and as a pastor of unabashed transparency and compassion.

Once Julian has given scope to the subjective side of our difficulties, she goes on – not to tell us, but to show us – how God loves us. And she does this in the same way that the visions were communicated to her: by presenting us with several striking images. In the richly enigmatic parable of the Lord and the Servant she discovers, after twenty years of meditation, the union between Christ and the human race which resolves the problem of judgement. In the figure of Christ crucified, she sees God suffering both with and for his creatures. Thus contemplating the Passion, Julian is made one with divine compassion. And so also, in her own pastoral practice, this self-giving love is extended outward as Julian shares herself with her readers and enters imaginatively and sympathetically into their spiritual plight. Finally, in her exposition of the motherhood of Jesus, Julian discovers a forceful vehicle for dramatizing our theological coinherence with Christ. At the same time this image provides the emotional power to inspire that practical trust in God's love that is the only lasting solution for impatience and despair.

THEODICY AS PASTORAL ART

What is commonly referred to as the 'problem of evil' in Julian's writing is really the 'problem of sin' rather than the 'problem of pain'. Unlike either Job or Ivan Karamazov, that is, Julian is not particularly worried about finding a way to harmonize the suffering of innocent humanity with faith in God's beneficence: the classical problem of pain. What she seeks is rather a reconciliation of human sinfulness with faith in God's omnipotence.[5] The question for her is: why does God permit, not physical, but moral evil? If 'sin is the sharpest scourge with which any chosen soul can be struck', why does God allow Julian and others like her to persist in sin even when they want to be free of it? Why, in fact, does God tolerate the existence of evil at all?

Hence, in approaching the temptation to accidie, Julian digs down to the more encompassing issues which spiritual depression is likely to provoke – questions about God's ultimate power and providence, the significance of sin, and the meaning of judgement. From her personal and pastoral experience, Julian seemed to know that intellectual and speculative perplexities could pose a serious obstacle to spiritual growth. The individual 'problem of sin' cannot be addressed so long as the larger, cosmic 'problem of sin' is felt as a crushing incongruity.

As Julian struggles with these issues in the course of the *Revelations*, she evolves a method of theological wrestling that has implications for pastoral guidance as well as for prayer. At first glance, this may not seem at all obvious. For although Julian committed her visions in writing so they might serve as spiritual guidance, the *Revelations* do not present Julian engaged in the work of actually directing anybody. Yet someone is under direction in the *Revelations*, and that is Julian herself. Her director, so to speak, is Christ. So Julian's intense exchanges with the Lord function not only as a model of dialectical prayer, but also as a model for direction itself: a relationship characterized by full and open expression of doubt and dilemma in which Julian feels free to ask searching questions of God.

The problem of reconciling the existence of sin with God's sovereign providence emerges early in the *Revelations*. It is raised four times and in various ways. The initial crisis is precipitated by the third revelation, an intellectual vision in which Julian sees God 'in a point', by which she understands 'that he is present in all things' and 'does everything which is done' (11). As she ponders divine omnipresence and omnipotence, the enigma of sin arises in her mind. If God is the ultimate cause of all things, if nothing ever happens by chance, is God also the author of sin?

In this revelation, an answer comes to Julian through the visions themselves – or rather, in what is markedly absent from them. For in all the visions, she says, 'sin was not shown me'. Because she cannot see sin, not even conceptually, she concludes that sin is 'no deed'. In its blank negativity, sin cannot be considered a positive action of any sort. God cannot be the agent, the force behind sin, because there is no creativity in it – only nothingness. In other words, Julian here adopts the Augustinian explanation of sin as an absence of good. As mere privation, sin lacks that participation in Being which causes things truly to exist. God is the author of 'that which is', not 'that which is not'.

Here the matter stands until Chapter 27, where Julian turns from her earlier metaphysical speculations to consider sin in more personal terms. She remembers how often she has been troubled by her lack of spiritual progress; she knows that only sin holds her or anyone else back. As she considers the terrible power and consequences of sin, a further philosophical question presents itself: given God's foreknowledge, why did he not prevent sin from the very beginning? Could not sin and all its inevitable suffering have been avoided right from the start? Yet this very thought brings on another bout of spiritual depression, for Julian admits that she grieved over this matter 'unreasonably, lacking discretion'. The whole investigation begins to assume a pointedly personal edge. At stake is no abstract inquiry into the origin of sin, but the question of God's toleration of it. Can such a God be trusted?

And so, unlike the previous answer, the solution in this case cannot be restricted to fine distinctions in the realm of metaphysics. Julian needs personal assurance. The words of Christ, 'Sin is necessary, but all shall be well, and all shall be well, and all manner of thing shall be well', give her encouragement and comfort. Moreover, she has come to recognize something useful about the after-effects of sin. Just as Hilton could advise bearing sin's pain to the point of finding release from its psychological hold, so Julian comes to a similar insight. For even if sin has no objective reality, the pain it causes does. The suffering involved in the aftermath of sin is real enough, and has a positive capacity to induce self-knowledge, break down pride, and force us to that utter dependence upon God which is our truest and best condition. We might say that here Julian discovers the antibiotic potential of sin as an illness that contains its own latent cure.

Still, this solution does not satisfy Julian permanently, for we find her two chapters later asking God for a bit more insight, 'some plainer explanation', through which her mind might be set at rest. Again the response she records is framed in personal terms, with the specific

51

admonition that she contemplate God's work in the atonement of Christ. The argument put forth is one from proportionality: if Julian will meditate upon the atonement, she will perceive how much greater it is than Adam's sin. Since God has set right the worst of all evils through the sacrifice of Christ, Julian should be convinced that God will by the same means 'set right everything that is less'.

The issue finally comes to a climax in Chapter 32, when Julian ponders the situation of the damned. Since the medieval Church taught that those who die either outside the Christian faith or without charity towards others will suffer eternal damnation, Julian wonders how God's pledge that 'all shall be well' can possibly be fulfilled. Surely this is the ultimate test-case for the promise given in her visions.

Again Julian is assured that God 'shall make all things well', but she is also informed of a mysterious 'great deed' that God will perform on the last day by which he will keep his word. What that great deed is, how it will be performed, and whether there is universal salvation, remain none the less secrets known only to God.

Reflecting on her dialogue with God on the problem of sin, Julian occasionally sounds a note of regret for her persistent questioning. At such moments she brands her inquiry 'folly' (27). In fact, the whole episode serves to underscore for Julian the limitations of human reasoning. There are some things, she explains, which belong exclusively to 'our Lord's privy counsel' and, inasmuch as they do not pertain directly to salvation, are hidden from our understanding (30). Hence, out of obedience and reverence, we should attend only to that part of God's wisdom which has been revealed in Christ. Attempts to pry into God's secrets can be actually self-defeating for 'the more we busy ourselves in that . . . the further we shall be from knowing' (33).

Yet it would be a mistake to regard Julian's confession

of ignorance and presumption as an unqualified denial of the legitimacy of her question, the human urge to speculate about ultimate mysteries, or her bold searching through prayer. Her attitude is at least ambivalent since her inquiry, after all, brings no condemnation, but an answer. The soothing refrain, 'All shall be well', while admittedly inconclusive from a philosophical standpoint, is none the less satisfying in literary and psychological terms.

Thus Julian concludes this part of her theodicy roughly where her celebrated prototype in the Book of Job finished his: in an attitude of awe, chastened humility, and with a faith renewed by divine communication. By allowing her readers to share in this painful process, she makes it possible for them to participate in her sense of assurance and joy. Because the hard questions are asked honestly and directly, her repeated probings are, in the end, cathartic. In this way, too, she exemplifies 'dialectical prayer': a series of strenuous exchanges with God that work towards an eventual resolution.

IMAGES DIVINE AND HUMAN: THE SERVANT

After the problem of providence and the persistence of sin, we come to the other major speculative issue of the *Revelations*, the question of judgement. Briefly the problem is this. In the visions, Julian perceived that God assigns to us 'no manner of blame' for sin. She saw no wrath in God, but rather understood wrath as a human characteristic arising from 'a lack of power or a lack of wisdom or a lack of goodness' (48). Yet she knows from the teaching of the Church that sin is indeed blameworthy and deserving of wrath. How is she to reconcile these disparate attitudes towards judgement? For Julian, this question is even more central, even more critically related to the problem of spiritual despondency than was the earlier question about divine providence and sin.

The conflict Julian senses is no simple opposition between the rival claims of mystical vision and ecclesiastical authority. It rather represents a clash between the strength of her mystical insight and her deep sense of personal sinfulness, guilt, and remorse – feelings wholly in accord with the Church's ascetical teaching on the unavoidable consequences of sin. Should these impulses be entirely rejected, and if not, how are they to be understood? How is genuine contrition balanced against the temptation to despair that inevitably arises when sensitive souls perceive in themselves the continued tenacity of sin? Accidie is thus more than a temptation to be rejected. It is also a spiritual problem whose resolution depends, in part, upon a theoretical explanation. The difference between a true and false sense of guilt begins to emerge as the dilemma of conflicting judgements is resolved.

Even before she is given an answer, Julian seems to realize that, if certain necessary distinctions are made, the disparity between God's judgement and that of the Church might be bridged. As she writes, 'This then was my desire, that I might see in God in what way the judgement of Holy Church here on earth is true in his sight, and how it pertains to me to know it truly, whereby they might both be reconciled' (45). An heir of the scholastic method, Julian is confident that apparent contradictions between two sources of divine truth can be harmonized by the application of critical distinctions.

Unlike her inquiry into the workings of providence, Julian's interrogation of God concerning judgement produces no scruples or hesitancy on her part. Because she considers the answer to this last question a practical necessity in discriminating between good and evil, she believes it must lie somewhere in the sphere of ordinary revelation rather than in the 'privy counsel' of divine mystery. Her attention, then, is directed towards Christ, the personification of divine self-disclosure.

The reply comes in the form of a mysterious parable of the Lord and the Servant, located half-way into the *Revelations* in the longest chapter in the book (51). It is central to the *Revelations* in its position, and it is central in another sense, too, in that it provides a key to understanding the revelations as a whole. Possibly because of its importance, it was this revelation that gave Julian the greatest difficulty in interpretation. She tells us that she brooded on it for nearly twenty years before receiving 'inward instruction' about its meaning.

In her earlier venture into theodicy, Julian could not fathom the ways of God simply by applying logical analysis to them. But in her second attempt – the problem of judgement – she does break through to insight, albeit after two decades. The questions posed in each case were quite different, to be sure. Yet her mode of seeking an answer contrasts even more sharply. While abstract reasoning failed in the first instance, meditation bears fruit in the second.

It is significant that the answer lay buried in a cryptic parable. Through story and imagery, a wisdom can be disclosed that is not accessible to logic: the nature of divine love, and God's union with humanity through suffering. The parable itself is an extended image, a magnificent allegory representing a creative reworking of several biblical motifs including the Fall of Adam; the Suffering Servant of Isaiah; and the parables of the Prodigal Son, the Workers in the Vineyard, and the Treasure Hidden in the Field.[6] Its details should be savoured, but the essential story is that of a dignified and peaceful lord who sends his beloved servant on an errand. When the servant dashes off to perform his lord's will, he immediately falls into a ditch and is badly bruised. No one is there to help him, and he cannot get out of the ditch by himself. His suffering is compounded by mental anguish and confusion, as he thrashes around helplessly in his confinement. But the chief source of his pain, according to Julian, is his 'lack of consolation', stemming from his inability to see his lord. No fault or blame is assigned to the servant for the situation that has befallen him. Indeed, it was his very promptness that occasioned his stumbling in the first place (51).

Clearly this is a version of the story of the Fall. But if it is supposed to be the biblical Fall of Adam, there are serious problems here for orthodox belief. In the first place, the fall of the servant is described as tragic rather than as culpable. It is only because of his eagerness to do his lord's will that the servant stumbled into a ditch and suffered injury, not because of any fault of his own. In fact, Julian explicitly teaches that the servant's will 'was preserved in God's sight'. Certainly this is hard to square with the deliberate disobedience of our first parents.

It is also worth noting the resemblance of the servant to those suffering from spiritual depression. The servant, like all God's lovers, has fallen despite his good intentions and, like them also, he suffers from too limited a horizon. If proficients are apt to be preoccupied with themselves – their falls from grace, their subjective emotional state, their own injuries – the servant, too, 'like a man who was for a time extremely feeble and foolish paid heed to his feelings and continued distress'. His 'greatest hurt' was 'lack of consolation, for he could not turn his face to look on his loving lord'. Like those suffering from accidie, the servant cannot see for a time God's love for him.

What the allegory of the Lord and the Servant presents is not so much a retelling of the Fall of Adam as the story of the Fall of Christ; the story of one fall is superimposed upon the other in narration. The descent of Christ from heaven to earth and the Fall of Adam from paradise to misery are somehow the same story. As a rendering of the Fall of Christ, the parable represents an imaginative reconstruction of the self-emptying described in Philippians 2, the systematic divestment by Christ of his divine prerogatives and even his human dignity: 'He . . . did not count equality with God a thing to be grasped, but emptied himself, taking the form of a servant.'

Julian's parable reveals the essential unity of the first and second Adam. Since God knew from all eternity that his Son would become man, a 'true union' existed between God and the human race 'which was made in heaven'. And so, Julian concludes, 'When Adam fell, God's Son fell'. Adam fell from grace to sin, from life to death. Christ fell from heaven 'into the valley of the womb of the maiden' and finally into hell itself. 'For in all this,' Julian remarks, 'our good Lord showed his own Son and Adam as only one man. The strength and goodness that we have is from Jesus Christ, the weakness and blindness that we have is from Adam, which two were shown in the servant.'

Julian is not here relating the creation–fall–redemption story as we are used to hearing it, in historical, chronological sequence. Her allegory rather represents the story of salvation seen in retrospect, from the wisdom of hindsight. We are presented with salvation history from God's perspective, as it were, as an already accomplished fact. This, we may assume, is the most comprehensive way of regarding the human condition.

The parable dramatizes our redemptive solidarity with Christ and illustrates the Pauline doctrine of imputed righteousness.[7] Jesus stands with the human race in a miserable ditch, from which we cannot pull ourselves out. At the time we see ourselves participating in the righteousness of Christ so there is assigned to us, as the visions testify, 'no blame' for our sins. Through the dramatic

57

power of allegory, Julian exercises her pastoral art as she dispels the anxieties of those troubled by their persistence in sin. For if in seeing us, God sees only his beloved Son, the grounds for fearing God's wrath disappear. God looks at us as we are in Christ and sees us in our final integrity: sanctified, glorified, sinless. As Julian says, 'And for the great endless love that God has for all mankind, he makes no distinction in love between the blessed soul of Christ and the least soul that will be saved' (54).

The parable shows that sin may be regarded from either an eternal or a temporal aspect. *Sub specie aeternitatis*, the Old and the New Adam are one. Christ and the human race are inseparable. From the standpoint of humanly experienced time, however, we are indeed chronically sinful and so in need of repentance and confession. Thus, both the teaching of the Church and that of the visions are found to be true, each corresponding to a distinct level of reality, and each addressing itself to a different aspect of our spiritual need.

And so, even though we are subject to time, we forget our eternal identity only at the risk of falling into despair. To counter despondency, the parable offers a firm ground for hope in something beyond our sense of personal weakness: the final perfection of human nature in Christ. In the movement towards consummation, even sin has a role to play. Despite our confidence in salvation, the fact of sin makes us face our human frailty. Remembrance of past sin, as Hilton points out, helps us grow in contrition and purity of heart. As the occasion for deepened humility and trust in God, sin is indeed 'necessary'. Those anxieties about the damage done by sin that first prompted Julian's theodicy dissolve in the parable's eschatological outlook, a vision in which even in sin 'God works for good with those who love him' (Rom. 8:28).

IMAGES DIVINE AND HUMAN: THE CRUCIFIED

The identification between Christ and Adam in the parable is established for Julian through the figure of a servant. This image, like many in the *Revelations*, functions as a verbal icon, vividly disclosing something of God. But the servant-figure reveals even more than divine mystery; it presents truth about human nature as well. All of us are embodied in that injured and frail man: 'For in the sight of God all men are one man, and one man is all men' (51).

The parabolic servant thus reflects backwards to the vision of sacrificial love which opens and pervades the revelations – the figure of Christ crucified. Here again is an image that reveals both the divine nature and the human condition. That the vision of Christ on the cross presents Julian with a kind of epiphany – a sudden manifestation of God – is clear from the very first of the showings. In that initial revelation, a bodily sight of Jesus' head crowned with thorns, Julian perceives that the one who 'himself suffered for me' is in fact God, because 'where Jesus appears the blessed Trinity is understood, as I see it' (4). The insight is spellbinding. In it the universal human query, 'What is God?', is answered. Everything we might hope to apprehend about God is discoverable in Christ. He is God *pro nobis:* God's self-disclosure, his word. 'The Trinity is . . . in our Lord Jesus Christ.'

The seeming contradiction in a revelation of God crowned with thorns is matched by the incongruity of Julian's emotional response to it. Gazing at Christ's bloody head, she tells us 'in the same revelation, suddenly the Trinity filled my heart full of the greatest joy'. The yoking of God and pain in Christ produces in the compassionate onlooker a similar conjunction of opposites: the mixture of suffering and joy. Later, still contemplating the Passion, Julian mentions how she 'laughed greatly' to see the fiend overcome by it. The happy ending, the 'comic resolution' of the drama of salvation, moves her to an outburst of merriment. As a representative of the saved, her high spirits are universally apt. Julian understands cheefulness as a fit response to the victory over evil revealed in the Passion (13). Even Christ joins in the mirth when he reveals the 'joy and bliss of the Passion' as its fifth and final aspect (23).

The vision of the Crucified unifies conditions which are, to ordinary thinking, opposites: divine beatitude and human misery in Christ, joy and pain in Julian. Julian gives voice to the enigma when she describes the vision as 'hideous and fearful and sweet and lovely'. This harmony of discordant qualities in the showing suggests a further paradox, however, one contained within divine nature itself: 'that he who is highest and mightiest, noblest and most honourable, is lowest and humblest, most familiar and courteous' (7). God is at once majestic and abject.

As in the case of the servant, the Crucified embodies *kenosis*, divine self-emptying. If in Christ God reconciles opposites – nobility and lowliness, power and humiliation – the point of this union of antitheses *in* God is the union of humanity *with* God. What God offers us through the abnegation of his servant, through his crucified self, is access to divine love. With the sight of Christ's head bleeding, Julian tells us, came a spiritual vision of his 'homely loving' (5).

Julian delineates the familiarity or 'homeliness' of God with his creatures through still another series of images drawn, appropriately enough, from domestic life. God is thus our 'clothing, who wraps and enfolds us for love' – a metaphor suggesting both protection and nearness. With this image, the violence of love shown in the Crucified softens to simple, mundane availability – one more extension of divine incarnation through *kenosis*. In his yearning for us, God is not content to become human, to become a servant, to die painfully. He lets himself become as commonplace as a familiar suit of clothes.

Julian's imagery of divine abasement perhaps reaches its ultimate expression in her depiction of the process of bodily elimination as another example of divine providence. Since God 'comes down to us in our humblest needs', he does not 'disdain to serve us in the simplest natural functions of our body':

> A man walks upright, and the food in his body is shut in as if in a well-made purse. When the time of his necessity comes, the purse is opened and then shut again, in most seemly fashion. And it is God who does this . . . (6).

God presses into the furthest reaches of his creation, stopping at nothing – not even our most elementary physical functions – to pour out his love. And so from this first vision of Christ crucified Julian learns that the entire universe is saturated with the divine. To become as familiar as our everyday clothing and as humble as bodily elimination, God lowers himself into his creation through progressive diminishment and suffering.

The response to God's 'homely loving' ought to be a corresponding artlessness on the human side. God desires our trust: 'It is very greatly pleasing to him that a simple soul should come naked, openly and familiarly' (5). Yet we can only reach such intimacy with God to the extent that we can bear the divine degradation in Christ, as well as our own participation in his affliction.

At one point, Julian comes close to repudiating suffering for herself and for her God. While intense concentration upon the animated crucifix at the foot of her bed was causing her almost intolerable anguish, a 'suggestion' came to her – perhaps from her own subliminal consciousness –

to 'look up to heaven to his Father' instead. Might she find some other approach to God, one that would circumvent the crucifixion and give her the inner serenity for which she longs? The notion represents a temptation to transcendental religion. Since Julian has already learned that 'where Jesus appears the blessed Trinity is understood', it is not really God the Father whom she is being encouraged to seek. Instead, she is being tempted to give herself over to a god other than the one revealed in Christ: a god who neither suffers nor causes his lovers to suffer with him. In this way Julian confronts the susceptibility in herself to use religion to transcend pain and attain disengaged tranquillity. But she immediately recognizes how unfaithful to Christ such a decision would be. Rather than circumvent the Passion, she 'choose[s] Jesus' for her 'heaven': 'for I would rather have remained in that pain until Judgement Day than have come to heaven any other way than by him' (19). She accepts in love God incarnate, finding blessedness ('heaven') and suffering inextricably woven together in him.

As her visions progress, Julian realizes that Christ's pain is not limited to the historical crucifixion which took place outside Jerusalem. Although at first Julian comforts herself with the thought that 'he suffered only once' (17), she gradually perceives the deeper mystery that 'now he has risen again and is no longer capable of suffering; and yet he suffers with us' (20). Christ's torments will persist until the consummation of time. Christ suffers both with and for the members of his body on earth: with them, because he is indissolubly joined to them as their head; and for them, because he longs for them in love. The clarity with which Julian sees this aspect of divine compassion – literally, God's 'suffering with' his creatures – causes her to qualify in some significant ways the doctrine of divine impassibility.

The notion that God cannot experience change, especially of an emotional sort, from any external source or within his own self, is called in classical theology his 'impassibility'. Christian belief has traditionally affirmed this tenet of Greek philosophy, while holding it in tension with biblical conceptions of God, in which the deity does indeed manifest change. For even beyond the picturesque anthropomorphism of some parts of Scripture, Christian revelation modifies a strict notion of divine impassibility in its assertion that 'the Word became flesh' and so became subject to all the vicissitudes of earthly existence.

Like the Church fathers who wrestled with this difficult matter before her, Julian embraces both sides of the truth represented in orthodox formulations. With them, she first distinguishes between Christ's divine and human natures, assigning impassibility to his divinity and passibility to the 'works of his humanity'. On the one hand, 'in so far as Christ is our head, he is glorious and impassible'. Immutable blessedness belongs to the nature of God. Yet 'with respect to his body, to which all his members are joined, he is not fully glorified or wholly impassible' (31). The Incarnation makes a difference, and not just to us. Going beyond patristic formulations, Julian sees that it also affects God.

This momentous insight enters into Julian's discussion of divine impassibility in Chapter 31, near the end of her initial foray into theodicy, where she is troubled about the problem of sin. When Christ responds to her questions and doubts, promising that he shall make all things well, she applies this assurance, interestingly enough, back to him. She is comforted to learn that his thirst 'will have an end'. Earlier, in Chapters 16 and 17, she had encountered and graphically described Christ's terrible physical dryness on the cross. At this point, however, she is engaged in pondering its spiritual signifcance.

Julian understands this dimension of Christ's thirst to be his 'longing in love' for us. Because we are still in process, still en route to the Kingdom of God, Christ's thirst persists. He remains in pain because of his solicitude for us, and his longing will not be extinguished until the last day. So although mystical union with his members on earth causes Christ suffering, he suffers another, distinct pang of desire on our behalf as well. Julian perceives that this love-longing shown through Christ's thirst corresponds to an attribute of God: 'For as truly as there is in God a quality of pity and compassion, so truly is there in God a quality of thirst and longing.' In Christ, the impassible God suffers for love.

Yet there is another level of meaning contained in this vision of Jesus' thirst. Because all mankind is caught up into Christ, the vision once again helps explain our experience even while it reveals God. Christ thirsts; and because of our union with him, we thirst, too. The thirst we feel is our unsatisfied desire for God, just as Christ's spiritual thirst is God's painful longing for us. Christ's thirst is active and creative: it 'draws us up' to God (52). It is a thirst that instils in us the yearning for God.

This revelation pertains to Julian's pastoral treatment of spiritual desolation. Once we understand how Christ's thirst is communicated to us, we can begin to see why our own desire for God causes us pain. The union between Christ and the human race presented in her vision of the Crucified, like the identification between the first and second Adam of the parable, reveals an ontological foundation for these afflictions: we are one with Christ in his human suffering. Nowhere is this conjunction clearer than in Julian's teaching on prayer.

THE DYNAMICS OF PRAYER

In the second revelation, Julian watches Jesus' face discolour as he hangs upon the cross. His bruised countenance is subjected to numerous wounds and injuries; blood dries and cakes on one side, then the other. It is what Julian classifies as a 'bodily sight': a simple gaze upon a physical aspect of the Passion. For some reason, Julian's perception of this second revelation is a bit faint, and she finds herself wishing to see more clearly. But she is answered in her reason: 'If God wishes to show you more, he will be your light' (10).

In this quiet experience, Julian recognizes a token of the human search for the 'face' of God. In this life we see something of God, but our vision is usually dim. We want more light, a sharper focus, a plainer image. Sometimes God grants us greater clarity, but moments of divine illumination are never permanent. Why?

According to Julian, God draws us forward to himself by fulfilling our hunger for him only partially. We seek him because we desire him. Once our craving is eased, satisfaction is withdrawn, so we might burn for him ever more strongly. Speaking personally, Julian relates: 'I saw him and sought him, and I had him and lacked him.' It is the recurrent round of tasting, yearning, consummation, and loss which every lover knows.

But the sense of loss is in fact purely subjective. Although Julian regards this inevitable impression of incompleteness as 'our ordinary undertaking in this life', it is not objectively true. Though we feel a loss of God emotionally, God is in fact always near us.

To show how this is so, Julian is abruptly led in her imagination from the contemplation of Christ's face to the bottom of the sea. Even under the ocean, a place utterly inhospitable to human survival, God is still present. If someone 'could see God, as God is continually with man' in that region, he would know himself 'safe in soul and body' (10). God is available in all circumstances, however sterile or threatening to life. In this second revelation, we notice once again how a vision of Christ crucified develops into a meditation of God's omnipresence. God is in all our experience, even our experience of his absence.

Reflecting upon her frustration in viewing Christ's face only dimly, Julian insists that 'we see him continually, though it seems to us that the sight be only partial'. The sense of incompleteness whets the soul's appetite; but meanwhile, we do see God. Consequently, when Julian maintains that 'seeking is as good as beholding', she should be understood in more than a moral sense. 'Seeking is as good as beholding' not only because seeking God without a sense of satisfaction may in fact be God's will for us, but also because seeking *is* a form of beholding. The apprehension of God's absence is a particular way of seeing God: the vision of diminishment manifested in Christ. 'Jesus wished . . . to make himself as much like man in this mortal life, in our foulness and our wretchedness, as a man could be' (10). Is it any wonder, then, that when seeking a face such as this, the results will at first seem disappointing?

The seventh revelation, in which Julian undergoes rapidly alternating states of consolation and desolation, likewise has to be interpreted through the Christology of the *Revelations*. Some of the pastoral conclusions Julian draws from this startling experience of being tossed between dejection and joy 'about twenty times' are worth noting. She realizes first of all that personal moral evil is not necessarily the cause of her spiritual depression. Although Julian might have wondered why she 'deserved' desolation, she frankly admits that she did nothing during the revelation to provoke it: 'For in this time I committed no sin for which I ought to have been left to myself, for it was so sudden.' Despondency, therefore, may be neither a punishment nor self-inflicted. As in Hilton's night of the soul, such interior sufferings are not prompted by immediate personal sin, but are rather a state God occasionally permits for our growth: 'Sometimes a man is left to himself for the profit of his soul, although his sin is not always the cause' (15).

But if desolation is not deserved, neither is consolation. Delight in God is a grace, and this gift is God's ultimate will for us. Julian grasps the practical implications immediately: we are not to 'pursue' pain, but instead 'do all in our power to preserve our consolation'. When spells of interior oppression occur, we can accept them, confident that God 'keeps us safe all the time, in sorrow and in joy' (15).

Later in the *Revelations*, in her explication of the parable of the Lord and the Servant, Julian describes another set of oscillations: dying and rising. Drawing upon the archetypal imagery of the Paschal mystery, she delineates the spiritual consequences of the allegory: 'During our lifetime here we have in us a marvellous mixture of both well-being and woe. We have in us our risen Lord Jesus Christ, and we have in us the wretchedness and the harm of Adam's falling' (52).

So it is conformity to Christ, dying and rising, that explains Julian's seemingly erratic fluctuations in mood, crystallized in the seventh revelation. Her readers' distressing bouts with spiritual depression become intelligible, too, as a consequence of 'Adam's falling' which is coincident, after all, with Christ's descent. Because of Adam, we are 'afflicted in our feelings'. Yet this very affliction is a token of our union with Christ. Since Christ has shared vicariously in mankind's sin and guilt, Christians will participate to some degree in his redemptive sufferings. A sense of interior desolation is a result of the Incarnation.

A CIRCLE OF COMPASSION

From her first vision through to her last, Julian is shown a 'revelation of divine love'. Looking at Christ's head crowned with thorns, she recognizes in him the blessed Trinity. When God reveals himself, it is as afflicted love. Later, Julian discovers 'a great unity between Christ and us' (18) in the pains of the Passion – a unity whose origins and consequences are dramatized by the parable of the Lord and the Servant. Divine compassion, extending itself through unitive suffering, moves from the Trinity through Christ into human beings: 'We all stand in this way of suffering with him' (18).

Because the suffering of God is an expression of his love, those who love more, suffer more. After describing the appalling symptoms attending Christ's physical drying up, Julian notes its effects on herself: his pains filled her 'full of pains'. And why? Because 'of all the pains that lead to salvation, this is the greatest, to see the lover suffer' (17).

Julian has been drawn into God's own compassion. With him, she suffers sympathetically. It is her love for Christ that causes her anguish and constitutes her pain. She resonates with the distress of the beloved, recognizing also that 'all creation suffered in general' at the death of Christ. And what holds true for her own feelings of compassion, Julian extends to 'all his true lovers', and particularly to Christ's mother Mary: 'For Christ and she were so united in love that the greatness of her love was the cause of the greatness of her pain. . . . For always, the higher, the stronger, the sweeter that love is, the more sorrow it is to the lover to see the body which he loved in pain' (18).

The compassion of God issues in the Passion of Christ. For us, to be drawn into God's love will involve immersion into his sympathetic suffering: a circle of compassion that springs from the love within the Trinity itself, flows through

Christ, is felt throughout creation, and in Christ's lovers returns again to God. For Julian, St Mary, and those who respond to the revelation of divine love, union with God entails union with the Crucified. The tenth revelation presents this mystery through an image at once palpable and sublime: what later devotion would refer to as the 'Sacred Heart'. Here Jesus leads Julian's imagination into his open side to reveal 'a fair and delectable place, large enough for all mankind that will be saved' (24). Interpreted from the standpoint of the Epistle of the Hebrews, this showing might illustrate how we now 'have confidence to enter the sanctuary by the blood of Jesus by the new and living way which he opened for us through the curtain, that is through his flesh' (Heb. 10: 19–20). In effect, Julian sees the veil of the sanctuary momentarily lifted to reveal 'a part of his blessed divinity'. She discerns mankind safe in Christ, even though entrance into divine life and love is through a wound.

Julian's readers none the less have reason to feel more immediately oppressed by the weight and tenacity of their sins, and downcast by the instability of their religious affections. The revelations do not dismiss these feelings, but provide a rationale, compelling both theologically and psychologically, for their existence. Her parable shows that in this life, the Old Adam and the New coexist within us. Adam's fall hurts us emotionally, spiritually, and physically. Our humanity is clothed in the rags of the servant.

Yet it is just this abject servant whom Christ has become in the Incarnation. Paradoxically, it is our very feelings of estrangement from God, like the other pains which make up the human condition, that join us most intimately with the Crucified – indeed, which testify to the union with him that already exists.

In her earlier speculations, Julian had wondered whether God, from whom all things come, was also the source of sin.

Eventually, she decided that sin has no objective reality, no 'being' in the metaphysical sense. The pain produced by sin, on the other hand, is real enough. This pain we bear all our lives, and Christ bears it upon the cross.

In the course of her struggle with the problem of sin, Julian concludes that, although he allows evil, God directly wills only the good: 'For all that is good our Lord does, and what is evil our Lord suffers' (35). Her choice of words is telling. As Simon Tugwell has pointed out, in the context of the *Revelations*, what 'our Lord suffers' contains layers of meaning.[8] Julian refers not only to what God 'tolerates' (the translation of her most recent editors), but also to the evil Jesus suffers upon the cross. And these two meanings of 'suffer' are related.

God, Julian maintains, does not cause sin. But the consequences of sin, the pain it produces, do in a sense emanate from God. From the cross springs our experience of 'woe', just as the resurrection generates 'well-being'. Whether we happen to feel one or the other depends upon how God is showing himself to us on any particular occasion. Both constitute the Paschal mystery.

The vision of the Crucified, then, addresses aspects of Julian's probing into theodicy. The origins of sin remain an enigma, a quest that vanishes like the 'being' of sin itself. But to her question, 'Is God the creator of all that is?' an answer does emerge. Everything, even pain, has its origin in God. Our sufferings are not only of a piece with Christ's, they derive from his: 'because he shows us his suffering countenance . . . we are therefore in suffering and labour with him' (21).

There is consolation in this perspective. It suggests that suffering love is at the heart of God's creativity. It relieves us of the illusion that life ought to be free of pain, at least for God's elect. With respect to Julian's pastoral aims, it removes some of the speculative obstacles presented by

70

our baffling persistence in sin, with its resulting pain and spiritual depression.

But in the *Revelations* Julian offers even more for our comfort than a profound Christological interpretation of sin and suffering. For she learned from her experience of alternating moods that 'pain is passing' (15). Her final revelation, a vision of Christ gloriously reigning in her soul, completes the previous showings of the Passion and focuses them towards their final, eschatological end. As the representative of her fellow Christians, Julian can claim on our behalf that 'the place which Jesus takes in our soul he will nevermore vacate' (68). As a result, we are even now 'more truly in heaven than on earth' (55).

We know Christ under a double aspect, in his pain and in his glory. If for the duration of this life we experience union with him principally through suffering, nevertheless his blessedness remains our ultimate destiny: 'one blessed love now has a double operation for us; for in the lower part there are pains and sufferings. . . . But in the higher part there are none of these, but all is one great love and marvellous joy, in which marvellous joy all pains are wholly destroyed' (52).

IMAGES DIVINE AND HUMAN: THE MOTHERHOOD OF JESUS

Throughout the revelations, Julian applies her critical and intuitive mind to drawing out the meaning of the images she is shown. In her delineation of images such as that of the world as a hazelnut, of God as our clothes, of the servant, and of the Crucified, her intellectual acumen is coupled with the images' own evocative power. With consummate literary skill, Julian first presents these richly embellished images to her readers' imagination. She then probes their theological meaning, all the while leading us to use these images as she must have used them herself – as meditative windows into God.

As a culminating instance of Julian's imagery, we might ponder her celebrated portrayal of Christ as mother. Not surprisingly, Julian develops this theme in the aftermath of her visions of Christ crucified and of the parable of the Lord and the Servant. For these images are linked theologically. The image of Jesus as mother functions for Julian as a theological vehicle, but its affective strength also reinforces her pastoral intent to engender our trust in God. Her appeal is to both mind and heart. Where the parable of the Lord and the Servant and the visions of Christ crucified had revealed our union with Christ, the motherhood image develops this same unitive theme in other, more tender terms.

Julian proposes three ways of contemplating motherhood in God: in the creative foundations of our human nature, in the assumption of that human nature by Christ, and in what she calls the 'works of motherhood' (59). God is first of all our mother because he created us. God is the source of our being – the ground of our existence, as we might say. But Julian's sense of Christ's motherhood encompasses more than this. Because each of us has been created in the image of God, we enjoy a particular affinity with Christ. For if Christ is 'the image of the invisible God' (Col. 1:15), and we are created in God's image, then from the beginning we are made in the image of Christ. Christ is therefore the mother of our 'substantial nature' – our full human nature in which the *imago Dei* is the *imago Christi*.

Jesus may also be called our mother because he has assumed this human nature corporeally in the Incarnation. Just as we are composed of the same material stuff as our biological mothers, so Jesus is made of the same flesh as all humanity. In calling Jesus our 'mother' by virtue of the Incarnation, Julian wishes to underscore his physical solidarity with the human race. In this bodily connection to us Julian sees, as did the patristic tradition before her, the generative source of our salvation. Just as St Athanasius held that the very assumption of our human nature by Christ redeemed it, so Julian considers Jesus our 'Mother of mercy' in this second mode of his motherhood. For by taking on our 'sensuality', he has redeemed it.

Hence, the purpose of this incarnational motherhood is not simply union with the human race, but what Eastern Orthodoxy calls 'deification'. If Christ descended into the human condition, it was only so we might ascend with him into glory. Our mother Jesus therefore carries us with him into the very life of the Trinity. By the humanity of Christ we are incorporated into the Godhead. The motherhood of Jesus thus unites him physically with us and is the vehicle for the mutual indwelling of the divine and the human.

Finally, Julian draws out the devotional sense of our ongoing relation to Jesus when she considers him as our mother 'at work'. She depicts Christ in the successive stages and roles of motherhood: pregnancy, childbirth, nursing, protection, discipline, rescue and comfort. Perhaps no image could convey our indwelling in Christ more effectively than that of Jesus as a pregnant woman, carrying us within him for love, and bringing us to birth spiritually through his labour on the cross. Later, he nurses us into maturity by feeding us, as mothers do, from the substance of his own body; in his case, by the Eucharist. Like a wise mother, Jesus does not expose his child to only one technique of training during its consecutive stages of growth. Sometimes he will discipline it to correct its faults (60). On other occasions, he will comfort and cleanse his child when it is injured. We, on our part, are to trust him, for 'he wants us to show a child's characteristics, which always naturally trusts in its mother's love in well-being and in woe' (61). In transmitting her revelations, Julian has shown us why trust in God is natural – that is, in accordance with human nature. When we know that there exists no wrath in God, but only a mother's piety for her stumbling child, trust in God is our spontaneous response.

A COMPASSIONATE ART

The Revelations of Divine Love catches us up in a dynamic of love that first affects Julian, and then, through her pastoral and literary art, her readers. Eager to love God more, Julian wanted to share imaginatively and affectively in the Passion of Christ. As she undergoes the sixteen showings, her love is in fact immeasurably deepened. The blessed Trinity reveals itself as afflicted love, united through suffering to human beings and indeed to all creatures. Julian cannot view such a revelation as a disengaged spectator. The visions pull her into the passion and compassion of God, thereby transforming her. Her compassion then returns to Christ, as she feels his pains with him, and to his suffering body on earth, her 'even cristen'. For their sake she commits her revelations to writing. The circle of compassion proceeds outward to embrace others in its movement back to God. As Julian testifies of her visions, 'In all this I was greatly moved in love towards my fellow Christians, that they might all see and know the same as I saw, for I wished it to be a comfort to them, for all this vision was shown for all men' (8).

In her pastoral method, Julian embodies divine compassion as she enters into the situation of her readers suffering from accidie. Like Hilton, she begins by attending to actual experience. 'Some of us', she writes, 'believe that God is almighty and may do everything, and that he is all wisdom and can do everything, but that he is all love and wishes to do everything, there we fail' (73). Our inability to believe in the power of divine love triggers spiritual depression. As the sense of hopelessness gains ascendancy, we may wonder why God permits sin, whether we deserve divine wrath, and how everything can, in the end, 'be well'.

With sympathy and psychological precision, Julian delineates the emotional tangles and intellectual perplexities that spiritual depression is apt to provoke. To this end, she probes the problems of sin and judgement. Because her searching questions are framed in dialogue with Christ, she exemplifies a bold, even argumentative style of prayer that is actually an expression of confident intimacy. Here intellectual rigour turns to prayer, and speculation to pastoral art.

Having taken the difficulties of the spiritually depressed into account, Julian moves beyond personal subjectivity to seek a solution within the larger Christian vision. A purely emotional consolation, or a narrowly individual focus, cannot suffice for long. Julian offers the despondent a theological context in which they can ponder the significance of their particular sufferings. The vision of Christ in the *Revelations* form the substance of this theological discernment. The figure of Christ crucified focuses into one the human image of God and the divine image of humanity. Accordingly, we see the crucifixion not as an isolated episode in history, but as an epiphany of God's generative compassion. At the same time, we also see there the human race bound up in Christ's affliction. In this light the experience of spiritual despondency, of desolation in prayer – even of God's absence – testifies to our union with the Crucified. Where once we had thought that sin and desolation indicated the absence of divine power, if not divine love, the visions now confront us with a God whose shocking debasement overturns our very questions.

It is apparent that Julian's pastoral guidance has been inspired by first-hand experience. She is able to deal effectively with the problem of accidie because she was evidently troubled by it herself. Julian knows that the matter does not admit of a simple solution, but depends upon nothing less than a deeper apprehension of Christ. Of course, not every problem presented to spiritual directors needs to have been part of their own spiritual history. But it is essential that directors know for themselves how grace works in various circumstances. Above all, they should strive to lead their charges to direct encounter with Christ. For this task they must be willing, like Julian, to teach the ways of prayer, to expose their own difficulties when helpful to others and, finally, to communicate something of their personal vision of God.

If at first Julian was troubled by the problem of sin, she is eventually faced not only with the inscrutability of moral evil, but also with the scandal of a God who himself suffers. The visions baffle, then illuminate, and finally transform those who contemplate them. They begin with detailed depictions of Christ's torments, but the horror of Passion eventually gives way to awesome compassion. 'The most important point to apprehend in his Passion,' notes Julian, 'is . . . that he who suffered is God' (20). What *The Revelations of Divine Love* shows through its sequence of visions is this vision itself.

1   Edmund Colledge and James Walsh, 'Introduction', *A Book of Showings to the Anchoress Julian of Norwich*, I (Toronto: Pontifical Institute of Medieval Studies, 1978), 33–4. Marion Glasscoe, 'Introduction', *Julian of Norwich: A Revelation of Love* (Exeter: Exeter Medieval English Texts, 1976), p. vii. Some mss. give 8 May as the date of the revelations.

2   *The Book of Margery Kempe*, ed. Sanford Brown Meech and Hope Emily Allen, I (Oxford: EETS, 1940), 42, 1, 8ff.

3   Anna Maria Reynolds, 'Introduction', *A Shewing of God's Love: The Shorter Version of Sixteen Revelations of Divine Love* (London: Longmans, 1958), pp. xii–xiii.

4   Chapter citations are from the long text of *Julian of Norwich: Showings*, trans. Edmund Colledge and James Walsh (London: SPCK, 1978; New York: Paulist Press, 1978).

5   Robert H. Thouless, *The Lady Julian: A Psychological Study* (London: SPCK, 1924), p. 66.

6   Anna Maria Reynolds, 'Some Literary Influences in the *Revelations* of Julian of Norwich', *Leeds Studies in English*, 7 and 8 (1952), 22.

7   Deryck Hanshell, 'A Crux in the Interpretation of Dame Julian', *Downside Review*, 92 (April 1974), 86.

8   'Julian of Norwich as a Speculative Theologian', *Fourteenth-Century English Mystics Newsletter*, 9.4 (December 1983), 202.

4

The Negative Way of Incarnation:
The Cloud of Unknowing

Though the author of the fourteenth-century *Cloud of Unknowing* remains unknown to this day, it is not too much to say that he produced the most notable single treatise of mystical theology ever written in English. For this work helped revive for the Western Church, and in a vernacular language, a form of contemplation known as 'negative' or 'apophatic' prayer. And while negative spirituality has never enjoyed the same measure of popular appeal as its affirmative counterpart, it points towards an essential dimension of God and of the human experience of God. As such it has, in some form or other, attracted earnest seekers from every major religion of the world. Yet the dangers and difficulties of the negative way are so formidable as to demand pastoral guidance of the most mature and judicious sort.

Such a guide, apparently, was the author of *The Cloud of Unknowing*. Just where he lived remains uncertain, though the dialect in which *The Cloud* and six other probable works of his were written has led scholars to conclude that he belonged to a 'central district of the North-East Midlands'.[1] Details within the writings themselves suggest that he was a solitary of some sort, a priest, and a spiritual director. Although most of his works are addressed to a specific individual, he clearly recognized that they would be circulated among a larger audience, and he even provided instructions on how they should be read. He must have been well known in certain religious circles of his day.

Whoever he was, the author of *The Cloud* certainly did not invent mysticism. This mode of spirituality had been known to Eastern Christianity for centuries, with roots extending as far back as Clement of Alexandria and Gregory of Nyssa. Its classic expression, however, is embodied in the works of a sixth-century Syrian, who called himself 'Dionysius the Areopagite' – a convert of St Paul's mentioned in Acts 17:34. His true identity, like the *Cloud*-author's, is lost to us. But his successful use of his pseudonym, one closely associated with an apostle, gave his writings an almost biblical sanction in the Middle Ages. For the *Cloud*-author, 'St Denis' is the one whose authority validates his own rendition of the *via negativa*.

Most Christian theology is 'affirmative' or 'kataphatic'. It is based, most fundamentally, upon the belief that God has revealed himself, and uses creatures as vehicles for his self-disclosure. If no creature *is* God, every creature yet bears witness to its Creator. For the Psalmist, 'The heavens are telling the glory of God; and the firmament proclaims his handiwork' (Ps. 19:1), or, as the poet Gerard Manley Hopkins would write, 'The world is charged with the grandeur of God'. Nature is alive with divine presence, and so also is history, Scripture, and the Church. The supreme instance of God's enfleshment is of course the coming of Jesus Christ.

In its most developed form, the Christian *via affirmativa* yields a sacramental view of the universe, a vision which sees the whole world as a communicating symbol of the divine. And it takes a correspondingly positive attitude towards our use of created objects and beings as a means of reaching God. The suppositions of affirmative theology thus support liturgy, religious art, theological discourse, and all forms of meditation that make use of images or ideas. In practice, then, as in theology, Christianity is largely a religion of the affirmative way.

Yet some of our earliest Judaeo-Christian roots suggest certain dangers inherent in this way. The ancient prohibition against graven images reminds us of the perennial human tendency towards idolatrous image-making. God cannot be reduced to any of our notions, words, or physical images of him. He is always 'other', always transcendent. Without this negative insight, we fall prey not only to the grosser forms of idolatry, the gods of stone or wood, but also to falsely literalistic if not absurdly anthropomorphic readings of scriptural metaphor. Surely God is not a burning bush, a rock, nor even a space in the holy of holies.

Negative theology emerges from this recognition that God is always beyond – beyond our words, our ideas, even our experiences of the divine. In a short work entitled *The Mystical Theology*, Dionysius outlined a method of prayer based on this insight. It consisted of systematically negating every quality that could be posited of God. He begins by eliminating such patently mundane characteristics as corporeality, and he ends up denying even the properties traditionally associated with God – goodness, for instance, and wisdom. We can deny these attributes, too, according to Dionysius, because our human conceptions of them inevitably fall short of the supreme reality they are trying to signify. When at last we find ourselves bereft of all mental concepts of God, we enter a 'darkness of unknowing'. At this point theological method is transformed into prayer, because in this intellectual darkness we can be mystically united to the unknowable God, and possess a 'knowledge that exceeds understanding'.[2] The *Cloud*-author situates himself squarely in this tradition of dark contemplation. He was the first to translate *The Mystical Theology* into English, under the title *Hid Divinity*, and he consciously draws on him as a source for the negative methodology he is expounding in *The Cloud*.[3]

Yet many sincere Christians since the fourteenth century have wondered whether the recovery of this apophatic tradition should really be considered a gain. In his own day, the *Cloud*-author had to defend himself against charges that his teaching was abstruse and inaccessible to all but the highly educated (PC, 20–21).[4] More serious objections have been raised in recent years by those who see *The Cloud's* neo-Platonic roots as basically incompatible with Christianity. For such critics, apophatic theology involves an implicit denigration of the created order, including the Incarnation. The method by which practitioners of the *via negativa* seek union with God, they charge, deliberately circumvents the Church's sacramental and corporate life. They believe that because negative theology lacks this wholesome context, it inevitably neglects the concrete and social dimensions of Christian life, and leads to an impoverished social theology. Said to be narrowly individualistic and escapist, negative mysticism would seem to be more a Plotinian 'flight of the alone to the Alone' than a fully Christian journey into the Body of Christ.

Such reservations have to be taken seriously. Dionysius was clearly drawing upon a neo-Platonic tradition that was in some respects incongruent with a genuinely incarnational Christianity. Often enough in the Church's history, a false asceticism has advocated disengagement from human society and has censured legitimate natural enjoyments. Today, one at least has to question the motivation behind some contemporary interest in spirituality, especially in its more 'transcendental' modes. When our personal and global problems become overwhelming, are we seeking a temporary respite through meditative technique, or an energizing encounter with the God who is at the centre of all things?

Yet the *via negativa* ultimately converges with the *via affirmativa* in the recognition that God can never be fully grasped by the human mind. And just as there are several versions of the affirmative way, so there is variety in the negative. The *via negativa* is not a uniform phenomenon, but is expressed distinctively in diverse traditions. It takes on different contours in neo-Platonism, Zen Buddhism, and Christianity, for example. The task of the Christian theologian is to integrate the particular insight of negative theology with the larger vision of an explicitly Christian faith. This is precisely what the *Cloud*-author managed to do. His contribution to Christian mysticism lies in his perception that the *via negativa*, far from bypassing the Incarnation, is itself intrinsically related to it.

In *The Cloud of Unknowing* and some of his minor works, the author presents a version of the *via negativa* imbued with the mystery of Christ. It is not only that his spiritual method presupposes the ordinary disciplines of sacramental and liturgical life, or the common affirmations of Christian revelation. It is rather that, for him, the very process of praying apophatically involves a particular union with Christ crucified. While the special insight into the Passion for which Julian had prayed came to her through the affirmative way of visionary image, the *Cloud*-author's negative way also leads its practitioners into the sufferings of Christ. But just who is called to this way into God?

THE CALL TO APOPHATIC PRAYER

In the 'Prologue' to *The Cloud*, the author drolly enumerates those he hopes will never read his book. These include the 'worldly chatterboxes, . . . the rumour-mongers, the gossips, the tittle-tattlers and the fault-finders of every sort'. He also asks, in a more serious vein, that it be studied only by those with a demonstrated vocation to contemplative prayer. They are to have practised 'the virtues and exercises of the active life' for 'a long time'. They must be wholly converted, in intention, to following Christ in every respect.[5] In his final chapters, the author repeats these warnings, urging in addition that no one undertake this kind of prayer without the approval of a seasoned spiritual director.

Why this caution? To unsympathetic readers of *The Cloud*, the author's careful restriction of audience might reinforce suspicions that gnostic elitism or marginal orthodoxy underlie his teaching. But in fact the *Cloud*-author seems to have anticipated these reactions. By limiting his readership to those whose commitment to Christ was beyond doubt, and whose vocation to dark contemplation had been adequately tested, he hoped to avoid just such misunderstandings. His aim is not simply to defend himself against hostile allegations lodged by uncomprehending critics; he is also concerned to exercise pastoral responsibility in his recommendations. Since he realizes that his teaching is liable to misinterpretation, especially if read piecemeal or by someone without sufficient background for it, he directs his audience to read *The Cloud* straight through, and several times over, if possible.

His guidelines for the discernment of a vocation to apophatic prayer are quite specific. He recommends that the daily experience of prayer be examined closely. If someone continues to draw strength, insight, and refreshment from regular meditation, such a one should probably persevere in that way of praying and not attempt the exercise of *The Cloud*. Since the practices of affirmative spirituality – reflective reading, meditation, and prayer – are still proving useful, they should continue to be employed.

On the other hand, the mere absence of consolation and insight in prayer does not in itself betoken a call to the negative way. After all, periods of dryness and desolation are fairly common. Julian does not become an apophatic mystic when she feels the loss of God, nor does Hilton recommend a form of negative prayer in his night of the soul. Julian and Hilton remain affirmative mystics who at times experience frustration, distraction, and a sense of incompleteness when they pray. So, presumably, do most people.

For the *Cloud*-author the call to apophatic prayer is evidenced by two sets of circumstances. Those who aspire to negative prayer must first be long practised in the affirmative way; and their desire for non-discursive prayer must be persistent, indeed, overwhelming. One has to find that the longing for it 'goes to bed with you, gets up with you in the morning, accompanies you all day in all that you do, separates you from normal daily exercises by inserting itself between your prayers and you' (PC, 67–68). St John of the Cross would later refer to this phenomenon as a 'ligature' – literally, a 'binding' of one's ordinary mental faculties in prayer. When this occurs, the call to apophatic prayer ceases to be a choice, really; it is simply the only way left to pray. In describing the conditions indicative of this call, the *Cloud*-author wants to make sure that apophatic prayer is not undertaken prematurely. In all cases, the advice of a capable spiritual director should be sought, since a mere interest in, or attraction to, the negative way is not enough.

Unlike some present-day advocates of apophatic contemplation, who are willing to teach a technique of 'centering prayer' to anyone, the *Cloud*-author insists upon individualized discernment (PC, 64–68; C, 75). Today his pastoral discrimination still seems well founded. Taken out of the context of Christian theology and regular liturgical practice, it is hard to see how negative prayer could possibly be experienced as union with Christ crucified. Yet this is precisely what our author believes to be at the heart of dark contemplation, as we shall see. Practised in a religious vacuum, negative prayer is emptied of its spiritual significance and power, and reduced to a mere technique of 'transcendental meditation'. More seriously, those who venture unprepared into apophatic meditation may soon become bored with it, and perhaps give up prayer entirely. Or they may encounter destructive energies now released from their subconscious in the profound quiet of contemplation. Hence the *Cloud*-author's rule that we be guided by an experienced director, both in discerning a vocation to apophatic prayer and in interpreting its effects later on, continues to be sound pastoral advice.

A necessary ingredient in determining readiness for this prayer, then, is a thorough grounding in Christian piety and sacramental life, 'the common straightforward way', as the *Cloud*-author calls its. With infant baptism presupposed, auricular confession becomes the immediate sacramental preparation for contemplation. 'Not before they have cleansed their conscience . . . according to the ordinary direction of Holy Church' should those aspiring to the negative way begin their course (C, 28). Confession is a sign of sincere conversion to Christ, and one of the avenues by which contemplatives participate in the fellowship of the Church.

Another way is through fidelity to the divine office. Although their personal prayers have undergone a profound change, liturgical prayer continues on a regular basis. Indeed their recitation of the office is now more deliberate and reverent, since true contemplatives 'have more regard for the Church's prayer than for any other' (C, 37). The *via negativa* thus builds upon foundations set by the *via affirmativa*. Contemplatives do not abandon the liturgical and sacramental life of the Church, but instead draw more deeply from it through their experience of contemplation.

What is set aside, however, is the use of meditation. The author prohibits both intellectual, 'discursive' meditations involving theological analysis and affective, 'imaginative' meditations that draw upon external or mental images. This would mean, for example, that all the images in *The Revelations of Divine Love* together with Julian's reflections upon their meaning would have to be left behind, at least during the time of the exercise. For the abandonment of all forms of meditation marks the critical shift to the spirituality of *The Cloud*. Yet the author warns against embarking on this path too soon. Years of training in meditation will normally precede the transition.

Though he clearly favours apophatic prayer and believes it to be a special vocation, the reasons for his preference do not stem from any sort of anti-intellectualism. Indeed, he calls human reason 'a ray of God's likeness' and advocates using it for theological and meditative reflection. Such intellectually and emotionally rich prayer constitutes a step towards contemplation that cannot be circumvented: 'If any man or woman should think to come to contemplation without many sweet meditations . . . they will certainly be deceived and fail in their purpose' (C, 7). Theological meditations foster an intellectual readjustment to the supreme reality of God that forms an indispensable part of the process of conversion.[6] Affective prayer, as we saw with Hilton, summons and purifies our emotional energies. The *Cloud*-author presupposes all this background before one undertakes the more strenuous prayer featured in *The Cloud*.

TO STAND IN DESIRE: THE EXERCISE OF THE CLOUD

The young man to whom *The Cloud* is addressed has evidently passed through such a course of preparation, and has just begun living in solitude. Since he is under the author's pastoral care, he must have been well known to him. We do not know the precise way of life of either of these men — whether they were hermits, anchorites, or members of an eremitical order, such as the Carthusians. In his opening remarks, the author traces the evolution of his correspondent's vocation. It is because of the love God cherished 'in his heart' for him since he 'first existed' that he now finds himself called to solitude. He has been led to this state of life by a 'leash of longing': the desire for God created in the depths of his soul by God's desire for him (C, 1). From now on, he must 'stand in desire' all his life (C, 2).

The method of prayer set forth in *The Cloud* corresponds exactly to this core of desire at the heart of the contemplative vocation. For although their approaches to prayer differ, the *Cloud*-author is one with Hilton and Julian in stressing the motive force of desire. According to Hilton, it is our 'desire for Jesus' that pulls us through the long night of the soul. Julian, on the other hand, describes our continuous longing for God, a desire that is alternately satisfied and frustrated: 'I saw him and sought him, and I had him and lacked him.' In the exercise taught in *The Cloud*, prayer is wholly reduced to the essence of desire.

How does this happen? The author explains that when praying, the disciple is simply to direct his love towards God alone: 'have himself as your aim, not any of his goods.' He must deliberately put everything out of his mind, even particular thoughts about God. Not only must he hold in check all the usual mental wanderings that distract us in prayer; he is not permitted to entertain even religious ideas

87

or inspirations. No incident from the life of Christ or the saints, no reflection upon the attributes of God – his goodness, for instance, or mercy – nor any of the graces we normally pray for at other times, can now be considered. Instead, the disciple is to focus his attention on the simple fact of God without analysis or elaboration. His attitude is stripped and stark, a mere 'naked intent unto God' (C, 3).

This simplified prayer is not easy. Soon the practitioner will observe how all kinds of thoughts arise spontaneously in his mind. Most alluring, because so evidently good, are those devotional reflections he might be inclined to fasten upon as in meditation. But for those called to dark contemplation, even these ideas must be suppressed for a while and held under a 'cloud of forgetting'. To keep 'treading down . . . the awareness of all the creatures that God ever made' is, the author concedes, 'hard labour' (C, 26). The singleminded desire for God, as it turns out, requires enormous effort.

Yet when we turn away from thoughts about creatures and look instead towards God, we do not find much satisfaction either. For we discover a 'cloud of unknowing' situated between ourselves and God. This obstacle is a 'privation of knowing' – our sense of our own ignorance of God. We have forced all relative theological concepts *about* God out of consciousness in order to encounter the One to whom they point: the Absolute and Ineffable. But the search for God does not end when the mind is emptied. Instead we find ourselves then in the state of intellectual blankness that Dionysius called the 'divine darkness'. It is full of possibility, but we cannot engineer its grace. Only God can 'send out a ray of spiritual light, piercing this cloud of unknowing between you and him' (C, 26). Most of the time our satisfaction will consist simply in giving full rein to our yearning for God.

At the beginning of the exercise we are most aware of

its pains and deprivations. We are still ignorant, experientially, of God; and our sense of intellectual bankruptcy is compounded by the willed ignorance generated in the forgetting exercise. We find ourselves uncomfortably poised between the cloud of forgetting and the cloud of unknowing: between the things we know but have chosen to forget, and the God we have chosen but do not yet know.

As we face the massive obstruction to God presented by the cloud of unknowing, the strength of our affection is put to the test. We are to 'smite upon that thick cloud of unknowing with a sharp dart of longing love' and never give up (C, 6). The essence of the prayer is ceaseless longing, directed over and over again to the One who 'can certainly be loved, but not thought'. Energy is the mark of vehement love. As intense desire was once the sign of a vocation to contemplation, now it is the substance of prayer.

However, the author's vigorous application of the *via negativa* is not limited to his discussion of prayer. In his treatment of other pastoral issues he again insists on the overriding importance of affection directed pre-eminently to God. Just how he draws on the negative way for a fresh approach to typical matters of discernment is particularly evident in one of his minor works, *The Epistle of Discernment of Stirrings*.[7]

The letter is addressed to a man facing some hard decisions regarding his fashion of life. Should he live in solitude or in community? When should he fast? When should he seek silence? These are problems of practical discernment which, while requiring some translation of circumstance for present-day Christians, remain fairly common in spiritual direction. Sometimes the practices the correspondent enumerates can be helpful: at other times, not. Because he is free to make his own choices in these affairs, he feels uncertain about which course to take. For this reason he has sought experienced counsel. But as the letter unfolds, our author presents a surprising 'answer' to matters that 'are in themselves unimportant'. Yet his response remains consistent with his characteristic approach to the *via negativa*.

First he points out how all these things – silence and speech, fasting and eating, solitude and company – are good, yet none is really the goal of our lives. In the emotional turmoil of decision-making, we are apt to forget how relative these matters are. But if we humbly put these polarities on either side of our consciousness, we can choose instead 'something between them', which is God. 'For silence is not God, nor speaking; fasting is not God, nor eating; solitude is not God, nor company; nor any other pair of opposites. He is hidden between them, and cannot be found by anything your soul does, but only by the love of your heart' (DS, 34).

Thus he applies the negative methodology of apophatic theology to a practical case of discernment. Since God is neither 'this nor that', we are freed from absolutizing any of our day-to-day decisions. Only God can be our absolute choice, and when we have him, we will possess the wisdom to govern ourselves in the rest. If we work at the exercise of dark contemplation 'without ceasing and without moderation', promises *The Cloud*, 'you will know where to begin and to end all your other activities with great discretion' (C, 42).

This exercise of choosing God unceasingly is described in the first few chapters of *The Cloud*. In the remainder of the book, the author answers objections, gives examples, and helps with anticipated difficulties. Above all, he seeks to undergird the use of apophatic prayer by analysing its theological and psychological bases. Like Hilton and Julian, this spiritual director is also a teacher. He wants to show why negative prayer 'works' by exposing its anthropological foundation. If his readers can perceive how negative prayer is grounded in our very nature, they will perhaps be more inclined to practise it and more deeply engaged by it when they do.

The concept of human nature developed in *The Cloud* is based, aptly enough, on the biblical notion of creation in the image of God. With Hilton, the *Cloud*-author interprets our innate conformity to God through the Augustinian tradition. As we have already seen, in this scheme the three 'faculties' of mind, reason, and will constitute human beings as a 'created trinity'. Mind is understood as the psychic ground of intellect and will, the powers by which we are able to know and love. The *Cloud*-author, however, regards the potential of these faculties – and hence, the particular way we are conformed to God – in a manner peculiar to the medieval Dionysian tradition.

For this school of thought, God is 'incomprehensible' to the intellect. God can neither be understood nor united to the human spirit by means of our 'knowing power'. By this, the *Cloud*-author is not suggesting that we can know nothing whatever about God. He is not an agnostic, after all, but a Christian apophatic mystic. What he does deny is our ability to 'comprehend' God; that is, to 'take him in' intellectually. Since the mystery of God cannot be squeezed into the finite human intellect, it cannot be the locus for mystical union. The will, on the other hand, extends beyond itself in love. It is the part of human nature that is created open-ended. We can 'comprehend' God by love because, in the act of loving, God is not confined to our limits so much as we are brought into conjunction with his vastness.

There exists, then, a psychological fitness, a certain natural potential for the exercise described in *The Cloud*, that corresponds to the image of God we bear. We were created for union with God; and in unitive prayer, we experience this congruence between our nature and his. Because of our capacity for love, 'our souls are fitted exactly to him . . . after his image and likeness'. By divine condescension, God 'fits himself exactly to our souls by adapting his Godhead to them' (C, 4). The potential for apophatic prayer resides in our ordinary natural endowments.

The 'loving power' located in the will thus makes this exercise possible: 'By love he may be gotten and holden; but by thought, never' (C, 6). Accordingly, we need to recognize the limits of our 'knowing power' in order to advance along the *via negativa*. Sometimes modern readers take *The Cloud*'s insistence upon abandoning theological categories in this prayer as a bold step towards non-dogmatic religion. But in fact, as we shall see, *The Cloud* itself presents a highly developed theology of the negative way, one that in every respect presupposes orthodox Christian belief. Early in his book, the author explains the practical reason for this temporary suspension of our regular thought processes: 'As long as the soul dwells in this mortal body, the clarity of our understanding in the contemplation of all spiritual things, and especially of God, is always mixed up with some sort of imagination; and because of it this exercise of ours would be tainted' (C, 8).

Human knowledge inescapably depends upon sense experience; it is always 'mixed up with some sort of imagination'. Negative theology does not discount the validity of Scripture, creed, or affirmative theology generally, but it does remind us that the very processes by which we attain any knowledge of divine things are imperfect or, as the *Cloud*-author says, 'mixed'. Far from unorthodox, this modest assessment of the theological enterprise was fairly traditional. Commenting on another of Dionysius' works, St Thomas Aquinas, for instance, states that 'the highest knowledge we can have of God in this life is that God transcends anything we can think about him'.[8]

Apophatic prayer, then, recommends itself because it is suited to our natural constitution: we can love God, but we cannot 'think' God. The *via negativa*, moreover, offers an oddly intellectual appeal. Since it presses the fact of our mental finitude to its furthest practical conclusion, its own foundations are rigorously logical. To these psychological and philosophical arguments, the *Cloud*-author adds other, metaphysical reasons for dark contemplation, which are among the most compelling of all. He develops these ideas in a lengthy letter written some years after *The Cloud*, called *The Epistle of Privy Counsel*.

The Cloud has spoken poignantly of a suffering that afflicts contemplatives: the grief of self-awareness. For when all other thoughts have effectively been put out of the mind during prayer, the awareness of self usually continues to press upon consciousness. This is the last thought to surrender to the 'cloud of forgetting'. For those who are striving to know God as their deepest identity, the persistence of the ego is an occasion of frustration and sadness. Of course, they still cherish their existence; they have 'no desire not to be'. But they find themselves the final obstacle to experiencing union with God. Hence, 'he who knows and feels that he exists has a very special experience of sorrow' (C, 44).

Privy Counsel continues *The Cloud*'s teaching that self-awareness must eventually cause us pain if we are to attain perfect union with God. But for beginning contemplatives, *Privy Counsel* offers a favourable interpretation of self-consciousness, one that turns this unavoidable impediment to contemplation into its entry-point.

At the beginning of his letter, the author urges his correspondent not to forget, but to be conscious of his own existence as he seeks God. He is to cultivate an undifferentiated sense of self that matches his simple apprehension of God: 'So in this exercise think of God as you do of

93

yourself and of yourself as you do of God – that he is as he is and that you are as you are.' Just as he entertains no particular thoughts about God, but only a general loving awareness of his presence, so the practitioner should consider his own existence in the same diffuse way. Self-awareness can serve as the way into God because 'he is your being and you are what you are in him' (PC, 19). Because God is Being itself, permeating and upholding all that is, we most readily contemplate his presence as the ground of our own being.

At a later point in his letter, the author explains that he has moderated his previous advice about forgetting everything, even oneself, because of his client's 'lack of experience in spiritual awareness'. In order to help him 'climb up to it gradually', he lets him begin with a vague sense of self (PC, 51). 'To think in this way', he argues against unnamed critics of his counsel, 'requires little expertise.' It implies no esoteric knowledge or refined techniques. In fact, he adds with a touch of sarcasm, 'it is an attribute of the most ignorant cow or the most irrational animal . . . to be aware of its own individual being' (PC, 20–22). Certainly it is not beyond the capacity of a novice contemplative. Before he finishes his course, he will have to undergo a stripping of self-consciousness to become fully conscious of God (PC, 53). Awareness of God will eventually replace awareness of self. But in the meantime, the metaphysical foundations of the exercise which the author develops in *Privy Counsel* offer a less violent entrance into contemplation. The sheer Being of God can be glimpsed even at the start in 'the mirror of yourself' (PC, 18).

THE NEGATIVE WAY OF PURGATION

Among the meditations practitioners of *The Cloud*'s exercise must drop are reflections on their own sinfulness – not, however, because they have somehow attained complete freedom from it. The author recognizes that sin intrudes upon every stage of human life. We are never without at least some 'stirring' of sin within ourselves. Yet our deepest moral healing comes not through meditation on our 'own wretched state', as helpful and necessary as this may be, but through God's hidden work in the recesses of our souls. For the sake of this more radical purification, then, we can let remembrance of particular sins and frailties fall under the cloud of forgetting. Indeed we must hold these memories, like any others, in check so as to focus our attention solely upon God.

The author devotes considerable effort to explaining why the 'blind stirring of love' he recommends will destroy 'the whole root and the ground of sin which always remains in a soul after confession' (C, 28). He wants us to see that deliberate suppression of memories is not the same as denial. We are not being dishonest, impenitent, or presumptuous if we allow ourselves to ignore sin during this prayer. We are rather granting our essential helplessness to achieve purity of heart when we let God purge us from within. For in this exercise only the effort of forgetting is 'man's work'. The impulse of love, the strength of our desire for God, is in fact 'God's work' (C, 26). Although we have to practise ceaseless vigilance to keep our minds clear, the exercise of *The Cloud* actually demands an intrinsic passivity towards the activity of God: 'Let it be the one that works; you simply must consent to it ... Try to be the wood and let it be the carpenter; the house, and let it be the husbandman dwelling in the house' (C, 34). As intellectually strenuous as the forgetting exercise may be, the essential action in contemplation is performed by God.

Still the memories, regrets, and sense of despondency connected with sin are all apt to interfere. Our author seemed to know from experience that when the mind is quiet and emptied, painful and disturbing impressions can spring up from the subconscious to the conscious mind. Even though he advises pressing these thoughts back under the cloud of forgetting, it is precisely with the purification of what we would call the subconscious that he is concerned. For he maintains that this exercise not only purges us of personal sin but also frees us of the 'pain attaching to it' – the same long-term 'effects of sin' that Hilton discusses in his *Epistle to a Christian Friend*.

Now we can see more clearly the reasoning behind the author's earlier counsel to seek sacramental confession before undertaking apophatic prayer. Only those who have already acknowledged their sins and been absolved from them can dare to forget them. To suppress memories of sin without prior confession would be tantamount to a form of psychological and spiritual denial, a resistance to repentance.

Most contemplatives, however, are more prone to be overwhelmed by personal sin than to refuse confronting it. Here, too, confession can be helpful. As in the case of Julian dealing with the spiritually depressed, or Hilton advising his scrupulous friend, the *Cloud*-author sees how confession provides an objective assurance of forgiveness. One who has been absolved can 'dispose himself boldly but humbly for this exercise', without fear of presumption.

To encourage those whose past infidelities make them hesitate to begin apophatic prayer, the author offers the classic example of the penitent turned contemplative: Mary Magdalene. This Mary is the composite figure of medieval art and literature – the woman from whom seven devils were cast out, the penitent who wept at Jesus' feet, the sister of Martha of Bethany, and the Mary who discovered the risen Lord in the garden. She stands, according to *The Cloud*, 'for all sinners that are called to the contemplative life' (C, 16). She quietly withstands her sister's reproaches for choosing the 'better part' of contemplation as she sits, listening to Jesus (Lk. 10:38–42). The vocation to contemplative life is thus liable to be interpreted as laziness by outsiders. But even more boldly, Mary resisted the temptation within herself to wallow in remembrance of her past sins.

The *Cloud*-author credits Mary with his own pastoral insight that past misdeeds are best forgotten. Far from delivering her to greater purity of heart, mentally rehearsing former sins would probably have the opposite effect: 'She was more likely by these means to raise up in herself a tendency to sin again.' So instead of dwelling on her sinful past, 'she hung up her love and her longing desire in this cloud of unknowing, and learned to love what she could not see clearly in this life' (C, 16). The message is clear. If Mary Magdalene, the notorious sinner of the gospels, could dare to forget her particular sins long enough to engage in apophatic prayer, we cannot suppose our own past disqualifies us from a comparable contemplative vocation. Therefore, the author concludes, all those called to contemplation, whether they 'have been habitual sinners' or not, have reason to hope that the purification they long for will come – not through endless remorse, but through the sustained application of love recommended in *The Cloud* (C, 34).

As we persevere in the exercise, we will feel more sharply the need for just such a liberation from sin. We have suppressed memories of personal sin temporarily during contemplation, but the fact of sin remains. More and more we sense that it obstructs access to full union with God: 'If you had God then you would be without sin, and if you were without sin then you could have God' (C, 40). Wanting God passionately makes us more sensitive to everything in ourselves that opposes him. As our desire for

God grows, we become all the more eager to overcome these last, largely involuntary pockets of resistance.

This longing, even impatience, for freedom from sin described by *The Cloud* is of a piece with Julian's insight that 'nothing hindered [her] but sin', or the sense of help-lessness portrayed in Hilton's spiritual night. For each of them, desiring God is coupled with loathing for whatever holds us back from him. Sin is the anguishing impediment that prevents union. Yet a crucial aspect of loving surrender to God involves relinquishing illusions about our sovereignty over our moral selves. Paradoxically, it is only by fervently willing God that we discover the insufficiency of will-power. Thus, in Hilton's spiritual night we cling only to our meagre 'desire for Jesus'. Julian finally gives herself over to a process of redemption that includes even sin. And for the *Cloud*-author our moral regeneration comes to pass not through staunch moral effort, but by letting God change us in a way entirely hidden from ourselves. During contemplation we are not allowed even to think of our sins.

But even if we manage for a time to put out of mind all memories of personal sin, the painful sense of ourselves as sinners may yet be overwhelming. In that case, the author allows a modification of the forgetting exercise not unlike the one he recommends in *Privy Counsel*. Just as in this later work he lets us think in a general way of our 'being', so in *The Cloud* we may ponder our sinfulness, not in its spec-ificity, but simply as our intrinsic state. This vague appre-hension of sin is still compatible with the exercise of forget-ting, though it is important to avoid analysing our sins. Their discrete elements should be rolled up in a single thought or word: 'Cry out spiritually, always with the same cry, "Sin, sin, sin", "out, out, out" ' (C, 40). On these rare occasions when words are employed in prayer, the author recommends such monosyllables as 'God' or 'sin', which sum up all that we love and hate. 'By "sin" you must mean some sort of undefined lump: nothing else, in fact, than yourself' (C, 36).

Unlike some recent interpreters of *The Cloud*, I do not think that these brief invocations are precisely equivalent to the mantras of Eastern or transcendental meditation. The author never suggests that they be used to induce meditative awareness. He is less concerned with his client's tranquillity of consciousness than with the integrity of his prayer. Words are uttered not in rhythmical incantation, but 'to give vent to his need and the labouring of his spirit'. This vehement articulation is more like a primal scream than a mantra. In fact, the author compares it to terrified shrieks for help – 'fire!' or 'out!' And as effectively as these cries bring human assistance, so 'short prayer pierces heaven' (C, 37).

Hence, when awareness of sin presses upon us during prayer, we can think of sin so long as we do not mentally dissect it but rather identify with it completely. We are the 'lump' that sin is. At the same time, we can use short, simple words to focus our summary apprehension of ourselves or of God. They give voice alternately to our desire for God and to our anguish over separation from him. At times we may find healing in the very exercise of 'longing love'; on such occasions, our interior rhythms of affection and distress become unified. For *Privy Counsel* the movements of contemplative longing and contemplative sadness combine in a single, memorable image of God as a medicinal salve: 'Take the good gracious God, just as he is and without qualification, and bind him, as you would a poultice, to your sick self, just as you are' (PC, 23).

With practice, the labour of dark contemplation becomes easier and even 'restful'. But at first this work is hard and toilsome. The clarity with which we come to see our sins causes almost intolerable pain (C, 69). Then there is the mental suffering brought on by intellectual deprivation. It has two sources: our ignorance of the essence of God, which we feel as the cloud of unknowing, and our willed divestment of knowledge, which constitutes the cloud of forgetting. When the mind is emptied of all particular images and concepts and forcibly maintained in a state of deliberate ignorance, it inevitably suffers. Reflecting on the purifying pain of these varied emotional and mental hardships, the author concludes, 'Truly this is your purgatory' (C, 33).

The purgation of the *via negativa* readies us for the joy of contemplative union – just as purgatory, in medieval theology, was thought to prepare saved but still imperfect souls for the bliss of heaven. But in the course of our labour along the way of purgation, we discover that this suffering is more than merely preparatory. It is itself a participation in the affliction of Christ. In the pain of self-emptying, we already have union with God.

THE NEGATIVE WAY OF INCARNATION

Those who pray in accord with *The Cloud* refuse to think about anything in particular during the time of their prayer. They will not entertain specific ideas about God. They do not even consider their own selves in this exercise except in so far as they simply exist, either as 'sin' or as 'being' in the Being of God. The 'self' has disappeared as a separately conceived entity over against God; true identity is found to be but an aspect of the divine: 'He is your substance but you are not his' (PC, 19). But to see ourselves in God is, as Julian learned from her visions, to find ourselves in Christ. The self-abnegation of the *via negativa* turns out to be the same way into God as the *via crucis*.

Here then is the real heart of the matter, though

interpreters of *The Cloud* have not ordinarily seized upon its profound Christology. Yet the very method of apophatic prayer witnesses to its Christic patterning. Its practitioners must ceaselessly empty themselves. Nothing can remain but love. This is the ascetical equivalent of *kenosis* – the divine self-emptying by which God becomes incarnate. If the affirmative way presents the rich content of the Incarnation, the negative way reflects another side of this mystery: the painful, costly process of Incarnation.

Apophatic prayer thus entails a conformity through spiritual discipline to Christ's divestiture of self. I think it possible to argue that for our author as for the Epistle to the Philippians, the progress of divine self-emptying leads inexorably to crucifixion: Christ 'emptied himself, . . . and became obedient unto death, even death on a cross' (Phil. 2:7–8). Commenting on the words of Jesus, 'if any man will come after me, let him deny himself, let him carry his cross and follow me', the *Cloud*-author asks, 'How, I pray you, can a man abandon himself and the world more completely, despise himself and the world more positively, than by disdaining even to think of the qualities of his own and the world's being?' (PC, 49; 51). For him, the forgetting exercise involves so total a 'death' to self as to constitute a particular participation in the mystery of the cross.

One who practises self-denying contemplation is thus intimately bound to the Passion. And like Christ's oblation of himself on Calvary, the effects of contemplative self-offering are both corporate and comprehensive. The practitioner 'is called upon to lift up his spirit in this spiritual exercise for the salvation of all his natural brothers and sisters, as our Lord lifted up his body on the cross . . . in general, for all mankind' (C, 25). The author maintains that no act of charity surpasses this one because none is closer to the source of grace (PC, 29). Since it is linked to the supremely generative death of Christ, the impact of negative prayer is felt in every sphere of existence. Its spiritual repercussions affect 'all people dwelling on earth' and, of course, the one engaged in this prayer (C, 3). This cosmic vision surely belies the familiar image of negative mysticism as solipsistic and life-denying.

Just as the fruits of contemplation reach the whole communion of saints because they are rooted in Christ, so the act of contemplation transforms those who practise it. In the course of their prayer, they undergo a remarkable change in their attitude towards others. United in spirit to Christ's universal sacrifice, they love all people without distinction. 'For the perfect worker here has no special regard for any individual, whether he is kinsman or stranger, friend or foe. For he considers all men alike as his kinsmen, and no man a stranger to him' (C, 24). Such instinctual charity would seem to constitute a 'reformation in feeling' comparable to the culmination of Christian life Hilton portrays in the *Scale*.

But for the *Cloud*-author it is the singular union with the cross occasioned by negative prayer which accounts for this altered state of consciousness. On other occasions, we may well feel a greater affection for some than others – a disparity that in no way mitigates our likeness to Christ since Jesus himself enjoyed special friendships with John and Mary and Peter (C, 25). Yet apophatic prayer characteristically expresses itself in unconditional love. According to *The Cloud*, this change in our inner dispositions during contemplation derives from the extraordinary union with the Crucified that occurs during this prayer. The universality of the cross extends, through the contemplative, to 'all people dwelling on earth'; and for a time catches up the one who prays in its all-embracing love.

Every authentic expression of human life is somehow part of the mystery of Christ. The enjoyment of natural affection, for instance, is sanctified by the earthly friendships of Jesus. The self-abnegating discipline of apophatic prayer shares in the universal dimensions of Christ's sacrifice on the cross. When engaged in the meditative exercises that the *Cloud*-author expects will precede dark contemplation, our focus is on the human aspects of Jesus. In negative prayer, on the other hand, we contemplate Christ's divinity. For in the house of the spirit, the author explains, Christ is 'not only the doorkeeper but also the door. He is the doorkeeper by his Godhead, and the door by his manhood' (PC, 56). The entrance to the Godhead is thus through the 'door' of Christ's humanity. There is no other route. Anyone who 'seeks to climb in to perfection by some other way', the author stresses, 'is not only a nocturnal thief but a daylight prowler' (PC, 58). In its articulated theology, goal, and method, the negative contemplation of *The Cloud* is emphatically Christological.

What is the relation between the 'door' and the 'doorkeeper'? At times, the author seems to enforce a gap between Christ's humanity and divinity. But at his best, he sees the door of the humanity opening into the wide mystery of the Godhead. Christ's human nature is what we look through, and what we go through, to discover God. Just as Julian passed from the contemplation of the physical aspects of Christ's afflictions to penetrate their spiritual meaning, so those following this progression in meditation gradually shift their attention from 'the suffering of his manhood' to 'contemplate the love and the goodness of his Godhead, because of which he stoops so low as to humble himself in our manhood doomed to death' (PC, 57).

God's self-emptying love makes negative prayer possible. Describing the natural faculties by which we can engage in dark contemplation, the author remarks that God 'fits himself exactly to our souls by adapting his Godhead to them' (C, 4). Even our creation in the image of God, our desire and capacity for union with him, depends upon divine self-abasement. The humiliation of the one who 'did not count equality with God a thing to be grasped' is present in the very work of creation.

A favourite text of patristic writers to explain the mysterious transition to apophatic contemplation was John 16:7: 'It is to your advantage that I go away.' Citing a sermon of St Augustine dealing with this passage, our author explains how forsaking imaginative meditation on the life of Christ – indeed, the abandonment of all intellectual satisfaction in negative prayer – is like the forfeiture of Christ's earthly form by the apostles. The apostles are 'loath to lose his bodily presence', while contemplatives cling to their engaging meditations on Christ's manhood (PC, 74–75). For both parties, the humanity of Christ seemed more palpable and comforting in earlier experience. Yet each is told that it is to their 'advantage' that the sense of Christ's physical presence be withdrawn. Why?

The Ascension is the final term of the Incarnation. When Christ recedes from human view, the process of *kenosis* is complete. For what could be more 'self-emptying' than to disappear? For Julian, the vision of Christ crucified led her to see that through divine abasement, God is everywhere. He is as accessible as a suit of clothes; he would be present to us even at the bottom of the sea. The Ascension, to which the *Cloud*-author appeals, represents the culmination of this process. 'He who descended is he who also ascended far above all the heavens, that he might fill all things' (Eph. 4:10). *Kenosis* and ascension represent but different aspects of the same divine movement into creation. In the 'negative way' of the ascension, Christ divests himself of individualized, tangible form to be present everywhere. The contemplative shares in both the self-abnegation of the kenotic process, and the glorification of the cosmic Christ.

'Nowhere bodily is everywhere spiritually', says *The*

Cloud, referring to the way its exercise should be practised. The author advises against traditional introversion as a method for undertaking this prayer: 'My counsel is to take care that you are in no sense within yourself.' Contemplation cannot be localized. When we engage in it, we should not imagine that our contact with God is taking place within, above, outside, or behind ourselves. The author deliberately leaves us 'nowhere'. We cannot hoard spiritual experiences within ourselves 'like a lord with his possessions'. Once again the method of prayer follows the pattern of self-emptying. If we are left 'nowhere' with 'nothing', our condition embodies the negative way of incarnation. When Christ reduces himself to nothing, he is manifested in everything. 'Our inward man', comments the author, calls this nothing 'All' (C, 69).

What the author of *The Cloud* has done, therefore, is to take the Dionysian tradition of negative prayer and shape it into a work of spiritual guidance. Influenced by medieval interpretations, he elucidates the role of ceaseless desire in our search for union with God. Where thought fails, love succeeds. His emphasis on love takes on deeper shades of meaning, however, as he develops the Christological foundations of 'this work'. Then the exercise of forgetting is seen to be part of the process of *kenosis*. The practitioner is united with Christ in his descent into creation through self-emptying.

The negative way of incarnation is full of paradox. While it can be apprehended experientially, it leaves the mind baffled. Even our inner sense of it eludes articulation: 'It is not a will nor a desire, but something which you are at a loss to describe, which moves you to desire you know not what' (C, 34). The mystery with which we are confronted can only be expressed through paradox: God is everywhere and nowhere; nothing and all. And in this conjunction of opposites, we can begin to see the convergence in Christ of all paths to God.

In her visions of the Crucified, Julian perceived the glory of God in the abasement of Christ: 'where Jesus appears the Blessed Trinity is understood.' The showings reveal a paradox within divine nature, 'that he who is highest and mightiest, noblest and most honourable, is lowest and humblest, most familiar and courteous'. Transformed by vision, Julian's interior response resonates with its contradictions. She feels joy and pain, consolation and desolation.

By a rather different route, the *Cloud*-author comes to a similar apprehension of the mystery of God. Julian's richly imaginative visions and his stark apophatic theology meet in the revelation of Christ crucified. While Julian meditates on these images and the *Cloud*-author suppresses them, the self-emptying love of Christ moves them both. The Christology of *The Cloud* explains how Christ is active in the exercise, even though he is not consciously 'thought'. Julian's *via affirmativa* and *The Cloud*'s *via negativa* illustrate how these two approaches to God not only complement each other, but coalesce in Christ.

1   Phyllis Hodgson, 'Introduction', *The Cloud of Unknowing and the Book of Privy Counselling* (London: EETS, 1944), pp. xlix–li, lxxxiv.

2   *The Divine Names and the Mystical Theology*, trans. C. E. Rolt (1940; rpt London: SPCK, 1971), p. 194.

3   The writings of Dionysius first became accessible to the Latin West through the labours of the ninth-century philosopher, John Scotus Eriugena. In the course of the Middle Ages, other translations of *The Mystical Theology* were made and commentaries written on it. Hence, the *Cloud*-author did not read Dionysius in the original Greek, but only through the interpretative medium of other scholars' work. Unlike Dionysius, medieval theologians

tended to stress the importance of love and desire in apophatic prayer – an influence clearly reflected in *The Cloud*.

4   Page citations of *The Epistle of Privy Counsel* are from *A Letter of Private Direction*, trans. James Walsh (Tunbridge Wells, Kent: Burns and Oates, 1965; rpt Springfield, Ill.: Templegate, 1979).

5   Chapter citations are from *The Cloud of Unknowing*, ed. James Walsh (London: SPCK, 1982; New York: Paulist Press, 1981). In a few instances I have departed from this translation by simply transliterating a Middle English word or phrase.

6   Evelyn Underhill, 'The Place of Will, Intellect, and Feeling in Prayer', *The Essentials of Mysticism* (1920; rpt New York: AMS Press, 1976), p. 106.

7   Page citations are from *The Discernment of Stirrings* in *A Study of Wisdom: Three Tracts by the Author of The Cloud of Unknowing*, trans. Clifton Wolters (Fairacres, Oxford: SLG Press, 1980), pp. 27–37.

8   *De Divinis Nominibus*, I, lect. 3 (Parma edn, XV, 271).

5

Epilogue:
The Vision of the Mystics

Social critics and educators have observed, and often bemoaned, the orientation of modern Western culture towards passive visual entertainment. The number of hours children and adults spend watching television and movies, now often without having to leave the privacy – and social isolation – of home, is an alarming index of our lack of creativity and increasing privatization. Yet even here, and in however a distorted form, the perennial human hunger for the Absolute manages to find expression. The accelerated violence and sensationalism of the media, the popularity of special effects, bespeak an unsatisfied longing for intensity of any sort – a deliverance from the drabness of workaday existence. In its better moments, science fiction portrays the open-endedness of human nature, our instinctive yearning for another world or Being that might complete us. Hence, the messianic mission of Superman, the quest for immortality in 'Cocoon', or the engagement with a wondrous Other in 'E.T.' or 'Close Encounters of the Third Kind'.

As the Church puzzles over her response to this yearning, do we draw upon the treasure represented by our mystics? Or do we seek to justify ourselves in terms of the ideal of productivity that has become for our culture the measure of all worth? Clergy and laity often find themselves caught in each other's escalating expectations. Always there are more discussions about ministry, more committees for ministry and even, occasionally, the actual work of ministry. The deeds of justice and mercy end up emptied of their spiritual power by the sterile activism that frequently motivates them. Rather than offer our world the vision given in the Book of Revelation – the transformed society of the heavenly Jerusalem – we limit ourselves to the ideals of secular ethics, even when we clothe these aims in religious language. We say we seek the 'Kingdom of God', yet we do not always seek the author of that kingdom, not God himself. Our situation is like that of Israel when God first addressed the boy Samuel: 'The word of the Lord was rare in those days; there was no frequent vision' (1 Sam. 3:1).

What the mystics can give back to us is this vision of God. They show us, and by the power of their literary art can make us feel, what genuine engagement with God is like. In one vision of Christ after another, Julian lets us see with her into the mystery of divine love. Here is Jesus' head crowned with thorns and covered with blood; there is the progressive drying up of his vital fluids. Here is an enigmatic parable; there a touching portrayal of Christ's motherhood. The world is held in her hand small as a hazelnut; and Christ reigns in the soul, never to vacate this chosen seat of glory. As Julian presents image upon image, we can no more remain neutral onlookers than she could herself. This is no passive visual entertainment. We are actively caught up in the process of transforming compassion to which her astonishing revelations bear witness.

Likewise the author of *The Cloud of Unknowing* presses us with him to his singleminded goal. Beginning with the compelling logic of negative theology, he urges us to the exercise of ceaseless desire, the beating upon the cloud of unknowing, that is his all-consuming passion. He wants God and nothing else: no idea of God, however exalted, will suffice instead. If God can be loved, but not thought, then the intellect will fast so love might have its feast.

In his *Scale of Perfection*, Walter Hilton presents a panoramic view of the mystical life. A shrewd psychologist and moral theologian, he discloses us to ourselves at critical points in our spiritual journey, signalling the graces that await us at every turn. Because Hilton speaks to our immediate state, untangling our moral and emotional dilemmas, we are helped to believe that holiness – harmony with God, harmony with others, and harmony within ourselves – is really possible. By bringing the vision of holiness before our imaginations, he shows us how the 'new gracious feelings' of a fully contemplative life might actually be experienced.

Thus, the pastoral art of the mystics consists above all in their communication of a vision. They remind us that those who embark upon the direction of others must themselves have glimpsed at least something of the divine and, like the mystics, be impassioned to share it. For Hilton, the hope of transformation; for Julian, the sight of Christ at one with our humanity in suffering and glory; for *The Cloud of Unknowing*, the conviction that apophatic prayer joins us to divine self-emptying – for each of these mystics the sense of profound hope they bring to direction is founded upon what they have seen of God. Their vision, at once shared corporately with the Church and felt with penetrating intimacy, serves as a never-failing source of confidence and joy in their direction of others.

As the mystics move from the apprehension of vision to its articulation, they invariably teach. All of them are concerned to draw out the meaning of what they have seen, so that theology follows inevitably upon vision. Julian's interpretation of the parable of the Lord and the Servant, for example, although separated from the showing by twenty years, is none the less intrinsically connected to the revelation. Once she perceives who the servant in fact is – that in him are bound up Christ and the whole human race – she goes on to explain how the parable applies to the practical problems of spiritual despondency.

Following as it does from vision, this teaching office also leads naturally towards the exercise of pastoral care. In our contemporary idiom, a 'pastoral' approach in ministry has come to suggest a 'non-judgemental' acceptance of another's standpoint coupled with a 'willingness to be helpful'. This line of thinking is utterly foreign to the English mystics. Though their pastoral practice is is authentically compassionate, their love has theological toughness and prophetic strength. Because they have seen God in vision and heard his voice, they can, like the prophets of ancient Israel, distinguish between true and bogus spirituality. It is out of love for his friend and in fidelity to the truth that Hilton rejects his friend's interpretation of prolonged contrition as evidence of divine wrath. The pastoral encouragement he would offer, like Julian's consolation for the spiritually depressed, is rooted in unsentimental adherence to theological faith. Only truth can finally comfort.

In much the same way, the *Cloud*-author harnesses the motive-force of reason to commend dark contemplation. He reinforces his description of this method of prayer with explanations of its metaphysical, anthropological and theological foundations. Even though the form of prayer he advocates is based largely on will and desire, he does not cut the intellect out of spirituality altogether. With Julian and Hilton he presupposes training in intellectual meditation; but even more, his pastoral writings themselves exemplify a balanced integration of thought, will, and desire.

Integration is in fact a hallmark of the English mystics, a distinctive trait of their pastoral approach. By contrast, we in the West are still feeling the rupture between theology and spirituality that took place in the early modern era. For us, theology can be a purely cerebral exercise, removed from its generative matrix of prayer, liturgy, and engagement with God at work in the world. On the other hand, what passes for 'spirituality' is often no more than the cultivation of subjective religious emotion, uninformed by disciplined theological thinking, corporate life in the Church, or the demands of justice in the world. Divorced from prayer and Christian practice, theology becomes abstracted and irrelevant; separated from theology and service, prayer becomes sentimental and self-indulgent. And what can we expect from pastoral practice when it is sustained neither by intense prayer nor by theological rigour but only by generalized good-will?

In their pastoral art, the English mystics show another way. With them, thought and feeling, desire and discipline, transporting vision and humble service, all coalesce. Working from theological premises, Hilton shows how our emotions can be used in prayer, why they do not have to hinder us when they go against our better instincts, and how they might be transformed. Julian also realizes that feelings, especially burdensome ones, require theological interpretation. For this reason, she presses the speculative questions of theodicy and judgement, which are finally satisfied only by a deeper apprehension of God in Christ.

Yet their intense consciousness of God does not render the mystics insensitive to individuals with their particular set of doubts and difficulties. They are not abstracted or 'other-worldly'. Attuned to the situation of his readers and correspondents, Hilton guides them through a theological understanding of their experience. His serene confidence in God casts a hopeful light upon the process of direction. The pressure of grace is always upon us, as God ceaselessly invites us to receive him whom Hilton calls both 'the giver and the gift'. The mystics are stirred to lavish their pastoral care on us because they have seen God at the centre of the cosmos, sustaining and regenerating it. Since the One they seek and love has poured himself out into creation through Christ, the cure of souls is scarcely an impediment to contemplation.

The vision of God, like the movement of grace witnessed in spiritual direction, is always a revelation. Whether in the arresting images of Julian or the austere negativity of *The Cloud*, we discover that God is not what we thought. He is everywhere because nowhere; homely yet the highest of all; unknowable and still manifest in Christ. By their pastoral art the mystics invite us deeper into this mystery, where our suffering and glory find their centre, and where wonder never finds an end.

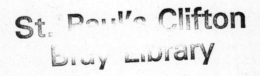

Select Bibliography

GENERAL WORKS ON THE ENGLISH MYSTICS

Knowles, David. *The English Mystical Tradition*. Tunbridge Wells, Kent: Burns and Oates, 1961; New York: Harper and Bros., 1961.

Pre-Reformation English Spirituality, ed. James Walsh. New York: Fordham University Press, 1965.

English Spiritual Writers, ed. Charles Davis. Tunbridge Wells, Kent: Burns and Oates, 1961; New York: Sheed and Ward, 1961.

Thornton, Martin. *English Spirituality*. London: SPCK, 1963; Cambridge, MA: Cowley Publications, 1986.

Pepler, Conrad. *The English Religious Heritage*. St Louis: Herder, 1958.

Fourteenth-Century English Mystics Newsletter, ed. Ritamary Bradley. Iowa City, Iowa, December 1974–83. Continued as *Mystics Quarterly*, 1984–.

The Fourteenth-Century English Mystics: A Comprehensive Bibliography, ed. Valerie Lagorio and Ritamary Bradley. New York: Garland Press, 1981.

WALTER HILTON

Primary Works
Of Angels' Song and *Epistle on Mixed Life*, ed. C. Horstman. In *Yorkshire Writers: Richard Rolle of Hampole and His Followers*, I. London: Swan Sonnenschein & Co., 1895, 175–82 and 264–92.

Translations

The Scale of Perfection, ed. Evelyn Underhill. London: John Watkins, 1923.

The Stairway of Perfection, ed. M. L. del Mastro. Garden City: Doubleday, 1979.

Minor Works of Walter Hilton, ed. Dorothy Jones. New York: Benzinger Bros., 1929.

Eight Chapters on Perfection and Angels' Song, trans. Rosemary Dorward. Fairacres, Oxford: SLG Press, 1983.

Epistola and Solitarium, trans. Joy Russell-Smith. In *The Way* (July 1966), 230–41.

'Epistle to a Christian friend newly turned to our Lord Jesu', ed. Clare Kirchberger. Under the title 'Scruples at Confession', *Life of the Spirit*, 10 (1956), 451–6, 504–10.

Criticism

Gardner, Helen. 'Walter Hilton and the Mystical Tradition in England', *Essays and Studies*, 22 (1937), 103–27.

Sitwell, Gerard. 'Contemplation in "The Scale of Perfection" ', *Downside Review*, 67 (1949), 276–90; 68 (1950), 21–34, 271–89.

Hughes, Alfred C. *Walter Hilton's Direction to Contemplatives*. Rome: Pontifical Gregorian University, 1962.

JULIAN OF NORWICH

Primary Works

A Book of Showings to the Anchoress Julian of Norwich, 2 vols., ed. Edmund Colledge and James Walsh. Toronto: Pontifical Institute of Medieval Studies, 1978.

Translations

Julian of Norwich: Showings, trans. Edmund Colledge and James Walsh. London: SPCK, 1978; New York: Paulist Press, 1978.

Criticism

Pelphrey, Brant. *Love Was His Meaning: The Theology and Mysticism of Julian of Norwich*. Salzburg, 1982. Elizabethan and Renaissance Studies, 92:4.

Llewelyn, Robert. *With Pity Not With Blame*. London: Darton, Longman and Todd, 1982. Published in USA as *All Shall Be*

Well: The Spirituality of Julian of Norwich for Today. New York: Paulist Press, 1985.

Molinari, Paul. *Julian of Norwich: The Teaching of a 14th Century English Mystic*. London: Longmans, 1958.

Reynolds, Sister Anna Maria. 'Some Literary Influences in the *Revelations* of Julian of Norwich', *Leeds Studies in English*, 7 and 8 (1952), 18–28.

Hanshell, Deryck. 'A Crux in the Interpretation of Dame Julian', *Downside Review*, 92 (1974), 77–91.

Tugwell, Simon. 'Julian of Norwich as a Speculative Theologian', *Fourteenth-Century English Mystics Newsletter*, 9.4 (1983), 199–209.

Bradley, Ritamary. 'Mysticism in the Motherhood Similitude of Julian of Norwich', *Studia Mystica*, 8.2 (1985), 4–14.

THE AUTHOR OF *THE CLOUD OF UNKNOWING*

Primary Works

The Cloud of Unknowing and Related Treatises on Contemplative Prayer, ed. Phyllis Hodgson. Exeter: Catholic Records Press, 1982.

Translations

The Cloud of Unknowing, ed. James Walsh. London: SPCK, 1982; New York: Paulist Press, 1981.

A Letter of Private Direction, trans. James Walsh. Tunbridge Wells, Kent: Burns and Oates, 1965; rpt Springfield, Ill.: Templegate, 1979.

A Study of Wisdom: Three Tracts by the Author of the Cloud of Unknowing, trans. Clifton Wolters. Fairacres, Oxford: SLG Press, 1980.

Criticism

Johnston, William. *The Mysticism of the Cloud of Unknowing*. 2nd edn Wheathampstead, Herts: A. Clarke, 1978; St Meinrad, IN: Abbey Press, 1975.

Egan, Harvey D. 'Christian Apophatic and Kataphatic Mysticisms', *Theological Studies*, 39 (1978), 399–426.

Knowles, David. 'The Excellence of *The Cloud*', *Downside Review*, 52 (1934), 71–92.

Dear Riders,

A warm welcome to Sunnyside Stables!

Sunnyside is our home and for the next week it will be yours, too! My husband Johnny and I have two children, Millie and James, plus two dogs ... and all the ponies, of course!

We have friendly yard staff and a very talented instructor, Sally, to help you get the most out of your week. If you have any worries or questions about anything at all, just ask. We're here to help, and we want your holiday to be as enjoyable as possible – so don't be shy!

As you know, you will have a pony to look after as your own for the week. Your pony can't wait to meet you and start having fun! During your stay, you'll be caring for your pony, improving your riding, learning new skills and making new friends. Add a trip to a horse show and a barbecue party at the end of the week, and you're in for a fun-packed holiday to remember!

This special Pony Camp Diary is for you to fill with your holiday memories. We hope you'll write all about your adventures here at Sunnyside Stables – because we know you're going to have lots!

Wishing you a wonderful time with us!

Jody xx

Sunnyside Stables

This map has been drawn by

DAISY

stables x 4

hay barn

stables x 4

feed room

barn

Dancer & Me

To upper fields →

Monday just after lunch

I'm so excited to be at Pony Camp! We've all been given these cool diaries to write about our week here and we're starting them straight away, sitting on the benches outside the farmhouse. It's been so fantastic here already and it's only the middle of our first day! I've been given a gorgeous pony called * **Dancer** * * and I'm sharing a room with these lovely girls, Isabel and Rosie, who are actually twins. How cool is that? I'd love a twin sister. Or any kind of sister, actually! I've got two little brothers called Jack and Ali and they aren't into ponies — they only ever want me to play Dinosaur Battles with them.

Isabel and Rosie are both 10 like me and they ride most Saturdays near where they live in Bath, which isn't that far from here. Well, not as far as Watford, where I come from, anyway! Even though they're identical twins you can easily tell them apart because they don't dress the same — well, they both wear beige jodhs, but Isabel's riding tops are pink and Rosie's are purple, and Isabel's a bit taller and they've got different hairstyles too. They've been riding for about six months and I only started a year ago, so we're really hoping we'll be in the same group. We had an assessment lesson this morning, all riding together, and the main instructor Sally's going to announce which groups we're in when we go back on to the yard.

Isabel

Rosie

pink

purple

10

In our room there are bunk beds and a single bed by the window. I arrived first so I got to choose and I went for the top bunk. Rosie's under me and Isabel's across in the other bed. We tucked our towels in under my mattress to make a secret camp in Rosie's bit, and we put the sweets and stuff we'd brought with us in a bag under her pillow, ready for a midnight feast!

SECRET CAMP!

hidden sweets!

I was a bit worried about making friends here, because of coming by myself, but Isabel and Rosie are really nice and it feels like I've known them a lot longer than, hang on, I'll just look at my watch — 3 hours and 41 minutes!

Here's a pic of *all* us girls squashed on to the benches, writing in our diaries. Sasha and Libby are both 10, like me, and they're sharing Millie's room. They're in the same riding group at their stables in Bournemouth and they came together. Millie's mum Jody runs Pony Camp so she actually lives here, lucky thing. She's 11 and so is Stephanie (who's sharing a room with Lara and Brooke, both 12). Stephanie, Lara and Brooke came on their own like me, all from different places I can't remember now.

When we'd unpacked and got our riding gear on, Jody took us down to the yard and introduced us to Sally, the main instructor, and Lydia, the head stable girl. Sally told us it's an especially exciting week for us Pony Campers because we're having a fab trip out tomorrow to a horse show. And guess what, her friend Kate is actually performing in it!

And that's not the only reason why this week is going to be extra-special! There's the big barbecue party on Friday too, which Jody mentioned in her welcome letter. It's the last week of Pony Camp for the year, so she's having the party to say thank you to all the people who've helped out this summer, like Western Bob and the lady whose beach they go riding on, and local farmers who let them have right of way over their land and the village shopkeepers who supply all the food. I can't wait!

After we'd introduced ourselves, we had a

tour round Sunnyside and that was brilliant because we got to see the ponies in the barn. We were all making a big fuss of them and wondering which ones we'd get. After that, we had a Safety on the Yard talk, and Lydia

pretended to do dangerous things like leaving an upturned rake on the ground and not shutting a stable door behind her, and we had to shout out "STOP!" and say what the mistakes were.

Then we all went crazy with excitement because it was time to find out who was going to be paired up with which pony. But we couldn't go round squealing and jumping up and down or anything, because Lydia was leading them out on to the yard and that would have spooked them.

This is who we got. I've made it into a puzzle for fun!

Sunnyside Stables

Lara

Brooke

Lucky

Charm

Fisher

Flame

Stephanie

Millie

Monsoon

Magic

Sasha

Libby

Amber

Hope

Me!

Isabel

Dancer

Rosie

15

Sally said Dancer is only here for this week, because she's looking after her for a friend's daughter while they've gone on holiday, so I'm extra-lucky to get her. She's so elegant and graceful (completely the opposite of me!) and she's really sweet too. When I took the reins from Lydia I gave her a big pat and she nuzzled into me straight away.

Here's my pony profile of her:

Name: Dancer

Height: 13.2hh

Age: 5

Breed: Maybe some New Forest pony in her, Lydia thinks!

Colour: Lovely bright palomino – I can't wait to groom her gorgeous mane!

Markings: Cute stripe down her nose

Fave foods: Yummy lush summer grass from the field

Personality: Elegant and graceful, and really friendly!

Everyone else loved their ponies too. In fact, there was so much cuddling and fussing and patting going on, Sally had to remind us a few times to mount up so we could get on with the assessment lesson!

We all rode into the manège, and Sally got us warmed up with loads of turns, circles and changes of pace. I'm a bit higher from the ground on Dancer than Bailey, the cobby pony I usually ride at my stables. And Dancer's slimmer as well, so it took me a while to get used to her and feel like I wasn't going to slide off! She's quite quick off the leg too – you only need to squeeze her into the next pace, rather than kicking on like I usually have to. I found that out the hard way when I asked for trot a bit firmly and she went skittering across the manège – I nearly *did* fall off then! Sally noticed but she told me not to worry, because the assessment lesson is *meant* for us to get used to our ponies.

I already felt extra-nervous riding in front of a new instructor and new girls, as well as on a new pony, so it was good to know she wasn't expecting to see anything amazing straight away!

Saying that, Isabel and Rosie looked really elegant and effortless on their ponies from the moment they got on. They both have really good seats and seem to change pace and direction without even *doing* anything. I can't believe they've only been riding for six months — I would never have guessed if they hadn't told me. I've been riding twice as long and I don't look like that!

It was really exciting when we all got to have a canter to the back of the ride. Dancer did a big plunge into it and I nearly came off again, but I grabbed the pommel and managed to steady myself and we made it round.

She was so graceful when she got going. Pity
I was bobbling around on top, trying to get
my balance – oh well!

Oh, hang on, Sasha and Libby are showing
everyone this cool routine they performed in
their dance school show. Isabel and Rosie want
us all to go and join in with it. I'm AWFUL at
dancing so I'm kind of pretending I'm too busy
concentrating on writing in here to notice, but –
EEK! – they're *making* me! Gotta go!

Monday still - in bed after lights out

Me, Isabel and Rosie are in the same group —
hooray! We've just been messing around in our
room after our showers and they've been trying
to teach me how to do a cartwheel. (I can *sort
of* do one, but I can't get my legs to stay straight
up in the air.) Theirs look brilliant
because they go to gymnastics
every week. That also explains
why they're such good riders
after only 6 months and why they were so
quick at picking up Sasha and Libby's dance
routine, when I couldn't get it at all. Honestly,
my feet were going everywhere (not that I
minded 'cos it was still loads of fun anyway!).

Before our lesson, we had a talk about tack
and tacking up from Lydia, and then we

practised on our own ponies in the barn. Millie
tacked up Magic in about one minute, and then
went round and helped everyone else – she's
probably done it about two thousand times in
her life! I always get to my stables a bit early so
I can tack up Bailey, so I was pretty confident
too. Dancer wasn't that keen on
standing still, though, so I gave
her lots and lots of fuss and
cuddles to keep her calm! And
she really jumped when the girth

strap accidentally slid off the saddle and swung
to the ground, poor thing, so I had to give her
another big stroke after that. She's so gorgeous,
I could just stay in the barn and make a fuss of
her all day! It's fantastic that I've got her for a
whole week, and that we really do get to do
everything for our ponies here, like tacking up,
grooming, mucking out and refilling their water
buckets – just as if they were our own.

At Isabel and Rosie's stables the tacking up's all done before they arrive, so they're not that confident about it. They did really well, but Isabel wasn't sure about getting the bit in, so I showed her this thing where you put your thumb in the corner of the pony's mouth.

"Wow, thanks, Daisy, that's a cool trick," she said, and I felt really pleased. And when Rosie got the throat lash twisted round the cheek piece on Amber's bridle, I just helped her undo it and start again.

The lesson was fab. Us three and Libby and Sasha are Group A, and we've got Jody teaching us. She makes things really fun and says "well done" a lot, so that's good! I'm glad she's not too strict because although I'm more used to Dancer being flighty now, I was still having some problems. Like, this gate clanged somewhere when we were trotting a twenty-metre circle and Dancer went skittering across the manège. I slid sideways and had to grab on to the pommel and pull myself up, which made me feel a bit flustered, especially because everyone else was still gliding round in these lovely flowing rising trots as if they hadn't even *heard* a noise!

Luckily, Jody just smiled and got me to trot Dancer round the manège to the other end, and then turn off the track at B to join the others. She reminded me to keep a really good contact through my outside rein and leg too, to keep Dancer on the circle and show her that I was in charge. That way if there was another noise, she'd be less likely to bolt off. I've never had to think about anything like that before, because Bailey tends to follow the track or the pony in front, but I will from now on, because I really want Dancer to feel safe and have confidence in me!

I tried really hard, and although Jody had to keep reminding me to sit up tall and look straight ahead (I think I was hanging on to the reins a bit and looking

Short reins!

down at my hands too much), things definitely got better. By the end of the week, me and Dancer should have it sussed, but still I'm glad we're having the barbecue party rather than a gymkhana or anything because I don't fancy trying to concentrate on all these new things while riding in front of a crowd!

It was so much fun in the barn after the lesson, because we got to give our ponies a really good groom down and get them fresh water and skip out the pens and sweep the walkways. Me, Isabel and Rosie made up this game where we pretended we were at pony

boarding school, and Libby
and Sasha joined in after
a while, too. It was
really fun and I wish
it was true life!

After tea and clearing up we all went
swimming (Millie's so lucky to have a swimming
pool and her own pony!). Us lot carried on
playing the boarding school game then too,
pretending we had to practise for the school
swimming gala. We put on posh voices and it
was *so* funny!

Right, my eyes are almost closing, so I have
to stop writing now. I can't wait for our trip to
the horse show tomorrow!

Tuesday at almost 9.30p.m. -
I'm writing this under the covers
by the light of my torch

What an amazing day! Our trip to the horse
show was fantastic! We've been so busy I
haven't had a free minute to write in here.

This morning after breakfast we got our
ponies in from the field. I was so happy when
Dancer came to me as soon as I called her, and
stood nicely while I put her head collar on.
When we'd tied our ponies up in the barn,
Lydia showed us how to check them over in
case they'd got any cuts or bruises in the field
overnight. Then she demonstrated how to give
them a really thorough groom, using
Lucky as the model. When it was
our turn to have a go, I spent ages
making Dancer's mane totally knot-free

and shiny (while telling her how gorgeous she is, of course!).

I helped Rosie pick out Amber's feet because there was a big stone right by the frog and she was worried about accidentally hurting her. Then Isabel was scared of brushing Monsoon's tail because she thought she might kick out, so I showed her how to put a straw bale behind her pony's hind legs, just in case.

"Thanks, Daisy," she said. "Where did you learn that?"

"Oh, just at my stables," I told her.

"You know loads about looking after ponies," Isabel said then. "You could be a stable girl when you leave school."

I grinned at her and said, "Wow, do you think so? I'd love that!"

Then it was time to get on the minibus to go to the horse show (we were having our lesson when we got back). On the way, we were all really excited, but we didn't know quite what to expect. We parked and walked across to the showground. It was a much bigger event than I'd imagined. There was this massive outdoor arena with seats all around it, and vans selling drinks and hotdogs and things. I thought we'd just be having home-made sandwiches or something, but Jody surprised us by treating us all to lunch. It was only half eleven, but we were hungry already. I had a burger and a fresh strawberry and banana smoothie that the lady whizzed up right in front of me. Delicious!

As we found our places, more and more people were pouring in, until almost every seat was taken. Isabel sat on one side of me and Rosie was on the other. It was so cool because

Brooke had some money with her and she bought two big packets of sweets (one jelly bears and one cola bottles), which she passed down the rows for all of us to share.

Well, the show was completely amazing! First a master horse trainer came on with four loose horses. The beautiful palominos (which looked like bigger versions of Dancer) were walking round him in a circle. Then he'd call one into the middle to do a trick like bowing, or even kneeling and then lying down and rolling completely over! The crowd loved it and the horses got treats from him after each trick, so they were happy too! When they all trotted out of the arena we gave them a huge clap, but we didn't know that the most amazing part of the act was still to come. One of the horses came back at a canter, reared up and twirled round and round!

29

It was so amazing, we all gasped and Rosie accidentally spat out a cola bottle!

After that, there was this really cute funny bit where a lady danced with her dog, then a showjumping demo, and some freestyle dressage and then, just when we didn't think we could see anything MORE amazing, the announcer said, "Ladies and gentlemen, please welcome the West Country's most daring duo, Kate Emerson and Starlight!"

That was Sally's friend! We all went wild, whooping and cheering when Kate came out on

this beautiful white horse with a lovely flowing mane and tail. She was wearing a spangly white leotard and ballet shoes, and Starlight had a feather headdress and a special saddle.

We could hardly believe our eyes as we watched their display. It was like gymnastics, but actually on a cantering horse! I didn't even know it was possible to do that! I've drawn some pictures so I can remember a few of the amazing moves!

Standing up on Starlight's back

Flipping off backwards

Doing a handstand on him! (I can't even do one on the ground!)

Kate told us later this is called the Flag Position

The announcer was right — they really ARE a daring duo. As well as all the breathtaking gymnastics, there were funny bits where Kate walked alongside Starlight and they both pointed their toes as if they were dancing.

And they crossed their legs over in time to the music, like this. ——

Then Kate ran next to Starlight and vaulted on for an incredible finale of Round the Worlds (not like the ones we do, but just on her arms with her legs flying in the air not even touching the saddle). Well, the whole audience went crazy after that, clapping and whistling. Kate took a bow in every direction (and Starlight bowed too — how sweet!). Then she turned to Sally, waved and did a bow especially for us, and everyone looked over! I felt so cool, being with someone who knows an actual famous person.

We didn't think the day could get any better, but something even more fantastic happened after that. As everyone started leaving their seats, Sally ushered us down too. We were expecting to go straight back to the minibus, but when we reached the front row she told us to go into it and sit down!

"Won't we get in trouble for sitting here?" said Sasha.

"What's going on?" asked Lara.

But Sally and Jody just grinned at each other, and Sally said, "Wait and see."

Then, would you believe, after a few minutes Kate and Starlight came back out again! We ducked under the barrier to make a big fuss of Starlight and told Kate how talented she was (well, the others did, I was a bit star-struck and nothing would come out of my mouth!). Of course, we all had loads of questions to ask her, and Sally got us to sit back down and stop talking over each other so Kate could actually hear what we were saying!

Lara asked about her special saddle and Kate explained that it's called a vaulting saddle, and that her show has developed from her training and background as a vaulter (vaulting is a kind of gymnastics you do on horseback). In an actual vaulting team there are 8 people, and they do all the tricks Kate did, as well as making human pyramids and throwing the littlest one (who's called the flier) up in the air a lot!

Kate said she started off as a flier when she

was only 7, which is younger than we are now!
Stephanie said she must have been really brave
to be thrown in the air from the back of a
cantering horse and Kate replied, "A lot of it is
about trusting your teammates. If you really
believe they'll catch you, you can do amazing
things – it's true that you still need all your
courage, though." Too right! There's no way
I would dare do anything like that!

Then Kate explained that you train for
vaulting on a lunge rein and she got Sally to
lunge Starlight while she showed us
the basics. You have to run next
to the horse and vault on and
then there are these moves,
including the handstand and
hands-only Round the World from
her display, that you need to show in any
competition. Apart from that, you can just
make up whatever incredible things you like.

Kate showed us her signature trick, a flying twist
in mid-air, which made us all gasp and go *wow*
again! When she vaulted off in front of us we all
gave her another huge clap. I really wanted to
ask for her autograph, but I felt too shy, and
anyway I didn't have anything with me for her
to write on.

I wish I could learn vaulting, because Kate
also told us it gives you confidence and self-
esteem, and improves balance, strength, poise
and grace – exactly what I need! She also told
us how important it is to be fit and flexible, and
got us up doing exercises in the arena! That was
so much fun – we did things like slow jogging
mixed with short bursts of fast sprinting, then
circling our arms, touching our toes and side
stretches, running backwards and sideways (that
was really funny because we kept banging into
each other and falling over!) and even leapfrog.

While we were getting our breath back,

there was a chance to ask some more questions. I got up the courage to say something then, because I was just so desperate to find out the answer and I didn't want to miss my chance. "Doesn't it make you nervous, performing in front of people?" I asked shyly. "Because I could never do it."

Kate gave me a big smile. "A few nerves beforehand are good, because they keep you on your toes," she told me, "but I know that during the performance I have to be calm and confident for Starlight. My stomach usually does a big flip just as I mount up, but we always enjoy it once we get out there!" I smiled back — I thought she'd say she doesn't get nervous at all, so it was amazing to think that even *she* does!

And I'm so glad I have her advice about that because...

guess what?!!!

We're doing our own riding displays at the barbecue party on Friday!

Eeeeeeeeeeeeeek!!!

Sally had been keeping it as a surprise and she announced it on the yard before our lesson this afternoon! She and Jody are going to help us make up fun five-minute displays in pairs (well, me, Rosie and Isabel will be a group of three).

Millie asked if she could do a handstand on Magic and then backflip off like Kate did and of

course they both said, "No!"

Millie went "Oh boo!" to that, which made everyone giggle.

We're going to use our lessons to work on our routines. I was excited about it, but I was also thinking, *how on earth am I going to perform in front of all those people?!* And Mum and Dad are picking my bros up from cub camp on the way here, so my whole family will be watching.

HeLp!

Although we'll only have our normal saddles and we can't do anything that daring (because you need to train for years and years to become as good as Kate and Starlight) Sally says there are plenty of things we *can* do. She told us to get thinking about themes too, to make our displays different from each other. Lara and Brooke are doing cowboys (well, cow*girls*!) and they're going to ride in checked shirts and jeans, and have cowboy music, and do a bit of line dancing at the beginning of their display before they mount their ponies.

Millie's pairing up with Stephanie, and they're being clowns and doing some juggling. Millie wants to do it while cantering, but Sally says that's not very likely!

Sasha and Libby are doing a dance theme and they're going to try and get their ponies to walk together up the school and halt and turn at the same time, and maybe even do some rein back, so it looks like *they're* dancing too.

Us three have decided on a gymnastics theme, and in the lesson Jody helped us come up with some ideas for moves, like trotting into the manège twirling ribbons, and bending round cones. Hopefully I'll be OK at it – I mean, I'm not exactly a gymnastics kind of person. When Isabel suggested doing Round the Worlds on just our hands like Kate did I thought HELP! But luckily Jody said no to that straight away. We are allowed to do normal Round the Worlds, though, and we're going to halt our ponies in a diagonal line across the manège and do them all in time with each other, so that should look cool.

We also had a go at vaulting on and off our ponies in trot, by just running beside them and throwing ourselves over the saddle then pulling

ourselves up. Isabel and Rosie made it on after
a couple of tries, but I couldn't manage it — my
arms just didn't seem strong enough. Also,
Dancer wasn't that keen on me suddenly
launching myself at her and she kept skittering
sideways, which didn't help. So we're going to
leave that out. PHEW! I really don't want to fall
off and look silly in front of everyone!

Sasha and Libby might put the vaulting move
in *their* routine, if they get more confident at it,
but they aren't sure at the moment. I hope
Isabel and Rosie don't feel annoyed that *we*
aren't doing it just because of me, though. Oh,
I'm sure they don't, they're so nice, and we're
doing loads of other cool things.

After tea we all hung out in the games room,
having turns on the table tennis and dance mats
and stuff, and Sasha and Libby worked out this
hand jive dancing bit they're going to do in
their display.

While we were waiting up here in our room for the shower to be free, Isabel and Rosie were trying to show me how to do a handstand properly (as in just in the air, without leaning your legs on a wall). They've got an idea that we could all dismount at the end of our display and do them in the manège. They can go upside down and stay there for ages, but even *with* the wall I'm not very good – my legs just slide down one way or the other after about a millisecond. I'm going to practise in every spare minute, though, so I don't let them down.

Oh, gotta go, I can hear Jody on the stairs. Goodnight!

Wednesday
I'm quickly writing this after lunch

Isabel and Rosie have gone to the tack room to
look through the box of show ribbons, to make
the twirlers for our display, but I wanted to stay
here in the kitchen and catch up with my diary.
Jody says we can try out the ribbon twirling in
our lesson this afternoon, but that if the ponies
spook we won't be able to do it. I'm worried
Dancer is *definitely* going to freak out. I hope she
doesn't because I don't want to let my friends
down and be the reason why we can't have
ribbons in our display (especially as we're *already*
not doing the vaulting on because of me).

ARGH! My mind's whirling
round and round with
all these thoughts now, and I'm getting more and
more nervous about the display.

This morning was really fun — up until our
lesson, that is! First we got the ponies in and
brushed them down (Dancer came trotting
straight up to me again and I was SO proud!).
Then we did a fitness workout — Sally had us
doing laps round Sunnyside and running to the
different markers in the manège. We all got the

Tee hee!

giggles during that, and Millie
and Stephanie ended up
having to lie down on
the woodchips because
their knees had gone
weak from laughing so much!

I helped Isabel and Rosie tack up again — only
with a couple of little things this time because
they're really getting the hang of it now. They
still said lots of thank yous though, and Lydia
said well done to me for being so helpful!
Dancer chose just that moment to nuzzle into
me, so I couldn't stop grinning. I gave her a big

hug and told her how fab she is, and how I wished she was my own pony!

It wasn't until our lesson went so badly that I started to get this nervous feeling. Here's what went wrong:

1. There's this bit in our routine where we get our ponies trotting down the long side, and then stand up in the stirrups and hold our arms out. We started with just a few strides of it and then tried to move up to nine or ten, but I could *not* get my balance and we had to keep starting again. I found myself saying "Sorry, sorry," to everyone because Isabel and Rosie could do it straight away, and also Sasha and Libby were waiting to practise their latest move and I felt like I was cutting into their time.

2. Dancer wouldn't stand still while we were doing our Round the Worlds – she kept walking forwards and I nearly fell right off! Also, it's even harder to do the handstand in the manège because your hands sink into the woodchips and put you off balance. Well, it is for *me*, anyway. Isabel and Rosie didn't seem to find it any more difficult. Help! I couldn't even do it in our room, and now it's even trickier!

3. I'm already worrying about the ribbons bit, even though we haven't tried it yet. At lunch just now, I wanted to say something to Isabel and Rosie about how I feel, but they were really excited about it and everyone else was saying what a fab idea it was, so I stayed quiet in the end.

Oh, they're back with the ribbons, so I'd better stop writing now and go and help make the twirlers.

Wednesday at 8.47p.m.

We've been swimming this evening and us three were first in the shower, so now we're lying on our beds in our PJs writing in our diaries while everyone else has their turn. Then we're all going down for our hot chocolate and to listen to

some of Jody's CDs and find a bit of music to go with our routine. I bet Isabel and Rosie are writing about how brilliantly this afternoon's lesson went (because it did go really well – for *them*) and about how much they're looking forward to doing our display on Friday. I'm glad they can't see what *I'm* writing, because the truth is that now I'm most definitely not looking forward to it **AT ALL**.

After lunch we went back out on to the yard and had a talk about points of the horse (well, pony!), colours and conformation, and then we went round looking at all the ponies and horses in the barn and stables to see what colours and markings we could find.

Everyone was chatting excitedly as we walked round, but I just started to feel smaller and smaller and quieter and quieter, and the horrible nervous feeling was getting stronger. I couldn't stop thinking about the ribbons and how Dancer might react. Isabel asked if I was OK, and I said yes and tried to smile more and join in after that, but inside I felt worse and worse.

By the time we walked our ponies into the manège for our lesson I was *really* nervous. Dancer seemed jumpy too – she even skittered about in the warm-up, and bolted off across the manège a couple of times when she was supposed to be trotting round the track. That made my heart pound even more, and when Jody got the ribbons out for us three to have a go at twirling I was absolutely dreading it. We started off holding the ribbons by our ponies' sides as we walked around the track, just to get them used to it, but even then Dancer kept snorting and swishing her head and stepping sideways away from the ribbons. I didn't think she'd like them – and I was right!

"Daisy, sit up straight, look ahead and be confident," Jody called. "Dancer needs you to show her that there's nothing to be scared of, but you look like a bag of nerves yourself."

I wanted to say, "Well, that's because I feel like one. I can't get anything right in this stupid display and I'm going to let everyone down and make an idiot of myself in front of loads of people." But of course I didn't. Instead I just nodded and bit my lip hard because actually, to be honest, I felt like crying.

Everything fell apart after that. Dancer wouldn't halt when we did the Round the

Worlds, so we ended up right behind Rosie
instead of nicely spaced out. And I could only

do four steps of the trotting
with my arms to the sides,
even though we had about
ten goes at it. And my
handstand isn't any better
than this morning.

It didn't help that Libby and Sasha's routine
looks fantastic (they're vaulting on and off, and
doing the hand jive while trotting now, when at
first they thought they'd only be able to manage
it in walk). And when I looked over into the
other manège, Millie and Stephanie were in
hysterics – they can't juggle *at all* at the
moment, never mind on horseback, but it didn't
seem to bother them. I wish I could just laugh
about the things I can't do, like they were, but I
couldn't. I didn't see Lara and Brooke's routine,
but from what they were saying at tea it sounds

amazing – they've got walk to *canter* in it, and even some leg yield! When I heard that I really felt stupid, because I'm the only one who's struggling.

Jody must have noticed how upset I was because she held me back at the end of the lesson and asked if I was all right. I said *yes*, but she then said, "You know, Daisy, you were so nervous when you came out here this afternoon, it's not surprising that things didn't go well. Dancer's looking to you for leadership – she'll have more confidence if you have a positive attitude. OK?"

I smiled and nodded, but inside I still felt like crying.

"Good girl," said Jody, "and don't worry, we all have off days and there's still plenty of time to turn things around before Friday."

She was being really nice, but I still felt awful!

When I got back to the barn with Dancer, Isabel and Rosie put their arms round me and asked what was wrong. For a moment I nearly told them the truth about how I feel, but instead I said I had a bad headache. They told Lydia I wasn't well, so while everyone was doing yard jobs, she let me stay in the barn and I had a big cuddle with Dancer.

"Oh Dancer, I'm sorry I'm so hopeless!" I sighed. "I just can't seem to get anything right in our routine. None of it's your fault, of course. I know I'm not a good enough leader to make you trust in me and that's why you're getting so spooked. I'm letting *you* down as well as Rosie and Isabel!"

 She whinnied gently and nuzzled into me as if to say she didn't mind, which was sweet, but I still feel bad that she's not having much fun.

"The problem is, I know what's wrong, but I have no idea how to fix it," I said then. "I mean, I can't suddenly become really good at gymnastics and be able to do all the moves by Friday, can I? And I can't ask Isabel and Rosie to change what we're doing – if we lose the ribbons and handstands and trotting with arms-out bits from our routine it's going to look completely boring!"

Dancer whinnied again and gave me a big nudge with her nose, and I knew she understood. I love her SO much! I wish I could be like everyone else, just really enjoying practising for the display and looking forward to Friday. It's all anyone's talking about and it's so hard to make myself smile and join in. Oh, what am I going to do?

Gotta go, Isabel's spotted something outside and she's calling us to the window. What's going on…?

Wednesday, really late at night!

Isabel and Rosie are asleep now. (Finally! We've been up whispering and scoffing sweets for ages!) But I can't settle down because everything that's happened keeps going round and round in my head. So I'm going to write it all down in here – thank goodness I remembered to bring my torch to Pony Camp!

Well, the reason Isabel called us over to the window was because she thought she'd seen a *ghost!* "It was there!" she insisted, tapping the glass. "A floaty white shape. By the apple tree!"

At first we thought she was joking, but she looked really pale and shaken, so we had to believe her – well, I believed she'd spotted *something*, anyway.

Rosie and I peered out too, but we couldn't see anything (it had got a bit foggy and it was nearly dark). I really wanted to see it for myself, but even though we stood staring out of the window for ages there was nothing, and it was getting darker and darker all the time.

"You must have imagined it," said Rosie finally.

"No, I didn't. I know what I saw," Isabel insisted. "It must have gone round the side of the farmhouse."

"Come on then, let's go and investigate," I said.

"WHAT?!" gasped Rosie, looking at me as if I was crazy.

"Perhaps it was just an old feed sack blowing in the wind or something," I reasoned. "But we're not going to find out standing here, are we?"

Rosie shuddered. "I'm not sure about this…" she began.

But surprisingly, Isabel was on my side. "Brrrr! I'm not going to get any sleep tonight unless we find out what that was," she said.

So then Rosie said, "Well, I suppose I'll have to come, then, won't I? I'm not letting you two go without me!" And that's how we ended up pulling our fleeces on over our PJs and heading down to the kitchen.

If Jody had been there, we'd have asked her if we could go out, but she was in the alcove bit in the hall on the phone. We hung around for a while, waiting for her to finish, but eventually we decided to quickly put on our boots and pop out to have a look. Well, I suppose *I* decided that, really. "I'm sure it's nothing and we'll be back in two minutes," I told Isabel and Rosie. "She won't even know we've gone." So we linked arms, holding on tightly to one another, and crept out of the door (Rosie remembered to put it on the latch so we could get back in again).

It was almost completely dark by then, and
in the rolling fog, Sunnyside seemed strange and
 – totally different from
the friendly, lively place
it is in the daytime. I wished I'd brought my
torch out with me, but it was too late to turn
back now. Our arms linked tightly, Isabel, Rosie
and I stumbled along, whispering and shushing
each other, while our eyes got used to the
dark. We reached the apple tree and, even
though going out there was my idea, I was
really relieved that we *couldn't* see anything
ghostlike. Then suddenly Isabel gasped and
tightened her grip on my arm. "There it is,
over there," she hissed.

We all saw it then, a white shape floating around at the far side of the manège fence.

I could feel Isabel trembling. "See? It *is* a ghost," she insisted.

"Let's run for it!" Rosie whispered.

But somehow I found a little bit of bravery and clamped my arms tightly round theirs. "We should try and have a proper look," I whispered. "Come on, it's OK, don't be scared."

They followed me and we tiptoed slowly closer to the shape. It was a misty white colour and really did look like a ghost.

"Told you!" Isabel hissed.

"Just a minute," I whispered. I listened out, concentrating hard. Yes, I thought I'd heard something that sounded familiar, and there it was again. "Erm, I don't think a ghost munches grass," I said then. "Listen."

We all stood completely still and silent, straining to hear. There was definitely a

chomping sound. And then the "ghost" did a
big snort! Of course! It was a loose pony!

We stumbled closer to it, and I spoke gently
so it would know we were approaching and
we wouldn't startle it. "Steady, boy – or girl,"
I said. "We can't have you wandering round
in the dark, can we? You might do yourself
an injury."

Isabel found a polo in her fleece pocket and
gave it to me. I made a clicking sound, held out
the polo and said, "Come on then, it's OK."
I was worried the pony might turn and bolt off,
which would have been dangerous, but he
came trotting towards us and took
it. Luckily, he had a head collar
on so I was able to gently take
hold of it. That's when we
worked out it was Charm. "He
must have escaped from the field somehow,"
I told them.

We weren't sure what to do next because it was pitch dark by then. We didn't want to lead him back to the yard in case he ended up injuring himself or spooking and bolting off, maybe injuring *us*. At first Isabel said she'd go and tell Jody he was loose, and get her to come with a torch and lead rope, but when it came to it, she was too scared to walk back to the farmhouse by herself. I realized that there was only one thing we could do – one of us would have to stay out in the dark with Charm. Rosie and Isabel said no way could they do that, they were far too scared. I was scared too, but I knew we couldn't leave Charm, so I somehow found myself saying *I* would do it.

"Wow, Daisy, you're so brave!" cried Rosie.

"We'll be as quick as we can," promised Isabel, and they linked arms and hurried back towards the farmhouse.

I stood holding Charm's head collar, patting

him and whispering that we'd soon have him
back in his field and everything would be OK.
Once or twice I started to get really spooked,
especially with the wind rustling the leaves of
the apple tree and making the branches creak.
But when that happened I just told myself firmly
that I had to stay calm and confident for Charm,
and somehow it worked.

I was relieved when I saw the
torchlight, though. "Over here!"
I called. It turned out to be Millie's
dad Johnny and James, her brother.

"Well done, Daisy," said Johnny, as he
clipped the lead rope on to Charm's head collar.
We walked along together, with Johnny's torch
lighting the way and Johnny leading Charm. "If it
wasn't for you girls he could have been out here
all night, running loose and maybe getting hurt,"
he added. "Although I think Jody will want to
know exactly *what* you were doing out here."

GULP! My stomach did a big flip then, as I wondered just how much trouble we were in!

Johnny and James walked me to the door of the farmhouse, and then they headed off up to the field to put Charm back. When I went into the kitchen all the girls were sitting round the big table having their hot chocolate. Isabel and Rosie looked relieved to see me, and Brooke said, "Oh, Daisy, thanks so much for finding Charm – he could have been badly hurt!"

But Jody turned round from the pan she was stirring on the stove and raised her eyebrows at me. "I'm so sorry," I blurted out. "Please don't blame Isabel and Rosie. Going out there was all my idea."

WHAT on earth were you thinking?

"What on earth were you thinking?" Jody demanded.

I blushed. It all sounded a bit silly now. "Isabel was sure she'd seen a ghost,"

I muttered, "and I just thought we should have a look. We were going to ask, but you were on the phone and we waited for ages, and we only meant to be out there for a minute so..."

Jody frowned. "Do you understand you're never to leave this house like that again without telling me?" she asked. "And the same goes for you too, Isabel and Rosie?"

She looked really cross and we all nodded miserably and said sorry again.

"I mean it, not even if you thought you saw a pink elephant juggling fire sticks," she added, smiling a little. Phew! So she wasn't *too* cross after all. Well, she was, but she knew we'd got the message. Then Johnny and James came in and told us that Charm had somehow managed to get the gate to the field open, and if it hadn't been for us then *all* the ponies could have been wandering round in the dark all night.

Jody said well done to us three then, for stopping a serious accident from happening (though she did tell us again that we should never have gone out by ourselves in the first place!).

We got our hot chocolate after that, and everyone wanted to hear the whole story, so we told them all the details. Isabel and Rosie wouldn't stop going on about how scared they were and how brave I was — well, I didn't think it was that big a deal, but everyone else seemed to!

When we were all in bed and the lights had been out for a while, Isabel and I crept into Rosie's bunk, and hung our towels down to make a secret camp. We got out our stash of sweets and started to tuck in. And that's when I found myself telling them how I feel about the display. I wasn't planning to, but it just came out. Somehow, after everything, I felt really close to them, and it was easier whispering it in the dark than saying it out loud in the daytime. I told them all about how frustrating it was not being able to get the hang of the moves, and how bad I felt for letting Dancer down by being so nervous when I should have been leading her. "Maybe I should pull out of the display altogether, tell Jody I'm ill or something, and you two can do it without me," I said. "I don't mind, honestly. I just don't want to spoil it for you by being rubbish."

"Absolutely no way," Rosie whispered. "It's one for all and all for one!"

"I wish you'd told us all this sooner," said Isabel. "I feel awful now, like we've made you do things you weren't confident about. If anything, *we've* spoilt it for *you.*"

"Of course you haven't!" I insisted. "I don't blame you two. I'm just really relieved you're not upset with *me.*"

They absolutely promised they weren't, and Isabel gave me her last drumstick lolly to prove it, even though they're her favourite. "You may not be confident about the display," said Rosie, "but you are in other things. Look at us two with our ponies in the barn, worrying about getting our feet trodden on and being nervous of putting the bit in! You're so confident you just get on with it, and you help us out too! And remember how brave you were tonight staying out in the dark by yourself."

Well, I hadn't thought of it like that before! I've been so busy concentrating on the things I'm not very good at, I forgot to see all the things I *am* good at! I guess sometimes it takes your friends to point the obvious out to you!

"Thanks, that means a lot to me," I told them. "But seriously, what are we going to do about the display? You're both so supple and balanced, and there's no way I'm going to suddenly be like that by Friday! But if we cut all the things I can't do out of the routine it'll look really boring!"

"Don't worry," Isabel said then. "I'm sure we can find a solution. Let's get some sleep and talk to Jody about it tomorrow."

So we scoffed the last of the flying saucers, and Rosie and I crept back into our own beds.

I feel so much better now I've told them the truth, and it's great that they've been so understanding. It's really nice of them to want to help me, but I still can't think of a solution. I guess I'll have to wait and see what tomorrow brings!

Thursday lunchtime

Wow, this morning went really well — much better than I could ever have imagined — and it was all thanks to Rosie and Isabel (and Dancer, of course!). After we'd got our ponies in and brushed them down, we all gathered round Jody in the barn to find out what our yard jobs were. Everyone was given theirs and went off to get started, except us three.

Jody gave me a smile and said, "Isabel and Rosie mentioned to me this morning that you're feeling nervous about the display."

At first I was a bit embarrassed that they'd told her, but then I was just relieved that I didn't have to pretend any more. "Yes, I am…" I admitted. "I'm sure it'll be fine, though," I added quickly. But I didn't sound very sure, not even to myself!

"Daisy, there's no need to put on a brave face," said Jody, "we're all here to help you. In the lesson this morning we can have a think about how to adapt the routine so that you're confident about it."

"But I don't want to spoil things for my friends," I mumbled, glancing at Isabel and Rosie.

"You're not," Rosie insisted.

"We want you to have fun and enjoy yourself, that's the main thing," Isabel promised.

"Are you really, really sure?" I asked.

"Daisy!" cried Isabel. "You have to believe us! I gave you my last drumstick lolly and everything!"

I grinned at them and they grinned back. What fab friends!

"Meanwhile, Isabel and Rosie have come up with some ways to help you improve your balance and confidence," Jody said then, "so instead of doing yard jobs, I'd like you to spend the next hour working together on that."

So that's exactly what we did! First they set up a line of straw bales down the middle of the barn and we all jumped from one to the other (the ponies were watching us, wondering what on earth we were doing!). When I got the hang of it they spaced them further and further apart. I really had to concentrate hard to keep my balance when I landed, and I fell off a couple of times. I did improve, though, and in the end they were so far apart that even Isabel toppled off at one point, so we thought we'd better stop there!

Then we all did the tree pose, which is this

yoga thing that they learned from their mum. The ponies were definitely wondering what was going on then!

After that we went out and tried some handstands up against the back wall of the stables. I did get a bit better, but my legs were still falling down sideways and I couldn't stay up very long before my wrists started to hurt. "I'm really sorry," I said, after about the fifteenth try, "but I don't think it's going to work, and in the manège I won't even have the wall and it's much harder to balance on the woodchips."

I started to feel a bit upset again, but Rosie said, "Don't worry about it, honestly, it is really hard when you're not used to it," and then Isabel came up with a fab idea of how to adapt the routine. So now we're going to all dismount at the end and walk forward away from our ponies, and then I'll jump into a star shape and they'll do their handstands up against me, so I'm holding their legs. Rosie thinks it will look even better than our original ending because they can stay up far longer with me holding them and I can count to five so they come down at exactly the same time, which will look SO cool!

TA-DAAA!

By the time we'd finished, I felt so much better. I couldn't stop smiling, and I told Dancer all about it while I was getting her tacked up for the lesson. When the ponies were ready, us girls went over to the manège and did a fitness warm-up with Sally again, which was really fun. Even when I got stuck halfway over Isabel's back in the leapfrog and we both fell down, I just collapsed in giggles. And the same thing happened to Millie when she was trying to leapfrog over Stephanie, so it's not like I was the only one.

Then we had to do the trust exercise of falling backwards and catching each other, which Kate showed us on Tuesday. I didn't think I'd dare, but I *do* trust Rosie, so I just let myself fall backwards (shrieking out loud as I went, but still!). And I made sure I stood really strong and solid when Isabel had to fall on to me, too, so that I didn't let her down.

Then it was time to get the ponies and mount up for our lesson. I was feeling so much more positive and confident, I hoped it would

rub off on Dancer too! I gave her a big pat
before I got on and told her how well we were
going to do today. She walked into the manège
really calmly and nicely and did the warm-up
without any problems. And she even stayed on
the circle we were trotting when Sally clanged
the gate of the other manège. It was working!

I really believed everything
was going to be fine, but
despite all my positive
thinking, when the ribbons
came out Dancer just
spooked again, as badly as last
time. She didn't even want them near her and
kept trying to go sideways to get away.

"OK, don't worry, Daisy," Jody called, seeing
me get a bit flustered. "You're focusing on the
ribbons a lot, which means Dancer will as well.
Just pretend the ribbon stick is a crop in your
hand and ride normally, as if nothing's different."

I nodded and gathered all my courage –
I really was determined to crack it!

Jody called out instructions and we all
followed, doing turns and circles and changes of
pace just holding the ribbon sticks like crops
(Sasha and Libby joined in with this as well, but
without the ribbons). It was tricky at first, but
Jody kept calling out new things and in the end I
just had to concentrate on those and I really did
forget I had the ribbons at all. Dancer seemed
to as well and in the end she relaxed and was
going really smoothly, and you wouldn't have
known she'd started off any more nervous than
Amber or Monsoon.

Gradually we started giving the ribbons a
little swish, but still by the sides
of us, not near the ponies'
heads or anything, and in the
end we could do quite large
circles without bothering them.

76

We're not going to ask for more than that,
though, as we don't want to push our luck!
We've adapted our routine slightly too, so that
instead of coming in swishing the ribbons
straight away, first we're going to walk the
twenty-metre circle just holding them, and then
we're going to do it again, in rising trot, swishing
them. There's a kind of intro bit on the music
we chose that's quite slow, and then as the
tempo picks up we'll start the trotting and
swishing. I was really pleased because that was
my idea, and Isabel and Rosie said they thought
it would look even better than before!

After that, Sasha and Libby worked on their
routine (which looks amazing, by the way!) and
us three got to join in with some of it. We had
a go at the dismount in trot and I managed it
OK, so we're putting that in our routine too –
after the ribbon waving we're going to leap off
and run alongside our ponies, and then hand

our ribbon sticks to Jody. As she takes each one, she's going to give us a leg-up back on, so I don't have to worry about trying to throw myself over the saddle – phew!

Seeing Dancer get over her fear of the ribbons gave me the confidence to be extra brave too! When we went back to practising our routine, Jody suggested leaving out the trotting down the long side standing up with our arms out, but it was actually *me* who said, "Could we try to adapt the routine instead? I think I can manage four paces." So we came up with the idea of Isabel doing twelve steps, and after four of them, Rosie joining in, and then after four more, me joining in. It looks really good, like a proper formation team, and you'd never guess that four is the most I *can* do! And when we do the Round the Worlds, we're *all* going to walk forwards, which means that no one will guess Dancer won't actually stay still.

Sunnyside Stables

So this is what our final routine looks like:

1. Enter at A in walk, ride 20m circle, ribbons still

2. Go rising at A. 20-metre circle, swishing ribbons

12. All bow. Da-daa!

11. Walk from F to K. At K turn in to face A in a row. Dismount and step forward for handstand finale

3. Circle again, dismount at F, run alongside ponies

4. Give ribbons to Jody at A and get leg-up. Go rising down KEH side

10. Walk across diagonal doing Round the Worlds

5. Stand up with arms out, me to join in after 8 paces from M

9. Canter to C/H corner then walk. Leave track at H and take diagonal through X

6. Leave track at A and take centre line, bending round cones

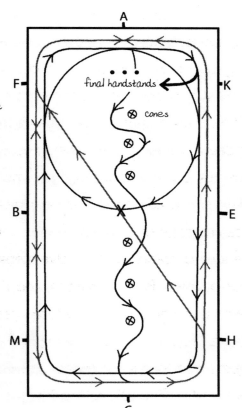

final handstands

cones

8. Go sitting in A/K corner and ask for canter

7. Join track at C, changing to left rein (don't forget to change diagonal)

79

Oh, looking back now I'm just so glad I was honest about how I felt – everyone's helped me so much, including Dancer. Having to be positive and help her get over her fears has given me the confidence to be brave myself and tackle the things I was scared of!

When the lesson ended, Jody told us all how well we'd done and I said a big thank you to her for helping me so much. "Oh, I didn't do a lot," she said. "It's you who helped yourself. I'm so proud of you for turning things around, Daisy."

Well, I was absolutely beaming with happiness then! And as soon as us three got back to the barn I gave my friends massive hugs and thanked them loads too! I can't believe how much things can change in such a short time if you really decide to have a positive attitude. I was dreading the display tomorrow, but now I'm really looking forward to it! And even better, I know my lovely Dancer is too!

Still Thursday

I'm just quickly writing this sitting at the kitchen table after our tea of jacket potatoes, beans and cheese – scrummy!

We had such a brilliant time on the hack out this afternoon. The straw fields have been cut now and the bales taken away, so there's just stubble left. We had permission to ride over it, too, instead of sticking to the paths at the sides as usual. So we all cantered over this entire field together and it was so exciting!

Millie went *galloping* off on Magic, and when Sally told her to slow down, she shouted back that she couldn't (yeah, right!). Then we did it again in the next field!

Dancer absolutely loved it and I didn't think about trying to balance or how to stop or anything, I was having too much fun! Jody noticed that too, because as we were walking along the track back to Sunnyside, she came up beside us on her lovely mare Bella and said, "If you can just relax and enjoy yourself tomorrow as much as you have today, the display's going to go fantastically!" And she's right! Of course I'm getting a bit nervous, it is in front of LOADS of people after all, but from what the other girls were saying at tea, everyone's starting to feel the same way!

OK, Brooke and Lara have finished now (they were on the clearing-up rota tonight) so Libby's put some music on and we're all going to hang out in here and help Jody prepare the food for tomorrow.

Friday, writing quickly just before the parents arrive

We're all ready for the party and everything looks fantastic. We've set up a long table outside the front of the farmhouse, and as well as the sauces and rolls for the barbecue, we put out all the lovely things we made last night. There are four different salads and three huge cakes (one carrot and two choc, which we got to ice

CaRRot Cake

ChoCoLate Cakes

and decorate – yum!) and a big bowl of our special tropical punch that we made up from all the different fruit juices Jody had bought.

It was so much fun helping with everything last night, while singing along to the CDs Lara had brought with her. Sasha and Libby made a huge "thank you" banner for everyone who's helped out with Pony Camp this year and it was so big they had to spread it out along the

hall so they could paint the letters. Then we all helped do horseshoes, flowers and stars round the edge. It's hanging above the door of the farmhouse right now and it looks amazing!

I think we look pretty amazing too! We're all dressed up ready for the display – us three are each wearing one of Isabel's pink T-shirts with our jodhs, and Lara lent us some hair mascara so we've got purple streaks in our hair! Sally said we could put some in our ponies' manes too, and it looks really cool. We've even taped a few pink feathers to the inside of their brow bands, so now they look like real performing ponies!

Sunnyside Stables

PERFORMING Ponies!

Libby and Sasha look fab in their leggings, legwarmers and slash-neck dance tops, and Sally found Lara and Brooke a pair of chaps each in the borrowing cupboard to wear over their jeans, so they really do look cowgirl-ish. But she said no to them wearing cowboy hats instead of their normal ones, of course!

I did feel a bit sad this morning as it was the last time I'd be bringing Dancer in from the field, but all the grooming, chat and fun this morning has really cheered me up, and there's still the display to look forward to. Our lesson was like a proper rehearsal — after the warm-up, we went out of the manège and stood by the fence with our ponies so that Sasha and Libby could have a few run-throughs of their routine, and then they did the same for us.

We went through it once with Jody calling out what was coming next from the piece of paper we'd given her, and then she put the music on her MP3 speakers and we had a go from memory. We all completely forgot what we were supposed to be doing the first time, but after that we got it into our heads and the next few goes went OK. We only managed to get the right number of strides each when we were standing up in trot down the long side *once*, but we agreed it doesn't matter too much as long as me and Rosie sit down again at the same time as Isabel.

Oh, people are starting to arrive… Gotta go! Fingers crossed it'll all go well!

Friday, back at home in my own room

I wish I could have stayed at Pony Camp for
ever! Today was the best day of all in the end!
Loads of people came to the barbecue party,
far more than I was expecting. And we all got a
big surprise when Kate turned up (Sally had
kept it a secret that she was coming!). We were
really excited to see her, but I felt even more
nervous knowing that she'd be watching our
riding display. In fact, by the time Mum, Dad
and my bros turned up, I was a total wreck!

When Sally stood up on a chair and
announced that we'd be putting on special
displays I knew I had to pull myself together –
and fast! I thought about how Kate had said that
even *she* felt nervous before a show, but that she
knew she had to stay calm for Starlight. I told
myself I had to do the same for Dancer and that

really helped. I also thought of how supportive
and encouraging Jody, Isabel and Rosie have been
to me and that made me feel a lot stronger too.

Well, us three were first up and when we
led our ponies out of the barn we saw that
everyone had gathered by the manège fence to
watch us. They started clapping as soon as they
saw us walking up, which was nice because it
felt like everyone was being friendly and wanted
us to do well, so it wasn't as scary after that. As
we mounted up and rode into the manège,
Jody reminded us to relax and SMILE! As she
went to start our music, I leaned down and
gave Dancer a big pat. "Just enjoy yourself,"
I told her. "This is our chance to shine!"

And guess what? It went really well (no, Dancer didn't shy at the ribbons and yes, we did actually get the right number of strides of the standing trot, and it must have looked cool, because everyone clapped after that move!). In fact, it was such fun that when we finished I wished we could have *another* go! Everyone went wild clapping when Isabel and Rosie came down from the handstands, and we all linked arms and took a bow.

It was such a wonderful feeling, doing our display and then seeing how much everyone had enjoyed it, and it's really made me want to do something like that again! Especially because I could see how proud Mum and Dad were. Even my brothers were staring at me with a look of amazement on their faces! Kate was clapping and cheering too, and later she said how well I'd done and that she would never

even have known I was nervous about performing if I hadn't told her! That just completely made my day! And yes, this time I grabbed some paper from the kitchen and

managed to get her autograph!

Anyway, we took another bow, ran up our stirrups and led our ponies out, giving them loads of praise and fuss (and the carrots Jody had handed us for them too!). We popped them into the barn and made it back to the manège in time to watch Libby and Sasha's display. It was great – they really are fantastic dancers as well as great riders, and they got a huge clap and cheer at the end, too.

Millie and Stephanie's act was completely different, but just as good. They were wearing

brightly-coloured clothes and had painted faces
and clown noses on. They did lots of funny
things like passing hand to hand and pretending
to try and push each other off. Millie actually *did*
fall off at one point, when they were pretending
to lose their balance as their ponies suddenly
went into trot. Everyone except us lot just

thought it was part of the
act, though, and she got
a massive clap for it!
And their juggling was a
disaster, but I think that
just made it even funnier!

Lara and Brooke were fantastic, almost like
professionals. Their whole routine was really fast

and daring, with lots of
cantering up and down
the manège and sudden
halts and speedy turns
and shouting *Yee-ha!*

By the end everyone was clapping along to their music, and when they finished they got the loudest cheer of all!

When we'd all done our displays, we got a *big* surprise because Kate came riding out on Starlight in a fantastic spangly show costume! They did the most amazing act, and everyone was gasping and going "wow" and clapping and cheering.

The party was brilliant, we all had loads to eat (and I had two slices of the choccy cake – yum!). I took Mum, Dad, Jack and Ali to meet Dancer and they all thought she was fantastic, and gave her loads of fuss and cuddles (even Jack, who's usually a bit nervous of ponies!). The party went on for ages and ages with music and dancing and all the lovely food, and none of us Pony Camp girls wanted to go home. We had to bring our suitcases down in the end, though, and start saying our goodbyes.

The mums and dads took some pictures of us all together, and then we had a massive group hug, and we gave Jody loads of hugs too, and then Isabel and Rosie both gave me hugs, and finally we went back to the barn and gave our ponies the biggest hugs of all.

I could hardly stand to leave Dancer, and I kept patting her and telling her how fantastic she was, and how brave she'd been about the ribbons, and how brave she'd made *me* too. Finally, Mum came in and said it was absolutely, definitely time to go.

Isabel and Rosie are going to keep in touch (in fact, as soon as we got home I was on Mum's laptop messaging them!). We're already planning to go back to Pony Camp together next year. And guess what? I've even decided to join gymnastics club after school. Now that's something I *never* imagined I'd say!

Love,

For the lovely Miss Daisy K xx

With special thanks to our cover stars,
Rachel and Toffee, pony guru Janet Rising
and our brill photographer, Zoe Cannon.

For loads of pony chat, visit:
www.kellymckain.co.uk

www.mandystanley.com

STRIPES PUBLISHING
An imprint of Magi Publications
1 The Coda Centre, 189 Munster Road, London SW6 6AW

A paperback original
First published in Great Britain in 2011

Text copyright © Kelly McKain, 2011
Illustrations copyright © Mandy Stanley, 2011
Cover photograph copyright © Zoe Cannon, 2011

ISBN: 978-1-84715-196-4

The right of Kelly McKain and Mandy Stanley to be identified as the author
and illustrator of this work respectively has been asserted by them in
accordance with the Copyright, Designs and Patents Act, 1988.

A CIP catalogue record for this book is available from the British Library.

Printed in the UK

2 4 6 8 10 9 7 5 3 1